VIETNAM & LAOS

ADVENTURES IN TRAVEL -- Winter 2006

Gary Brown

This journal was transcribed from the original hand-written journal maintained by Gary during his trip to Vietnam.

WEDNESDAY, NOVEMBER 22

Bloody Mary's at SeaTac to launch our trip

We are sitting in the Admiral's Club of Northwest Airlines at Seattle's airport looking out the window at the Airbus A330-200 that will fly us to Seoul, South Korea via Tokyo, Japan. We depart at 12:30 p.m. and will land in Tokyo in eleven hours. We have two hours at Tokyo's Narita airport and then have another three hours to Seoul; sixteen total hours which will make it 4:30 a.m. tomorrow Seattle time when we arrive in Seoul. However, it will be 9:30 p.m. Seoul time which is 17 hours ahead of Seattle's. By the time we get our luggage and get from the Incheon airport to our hotel in Seoul, it will be near midnight on November 23, which means we will have missed Thanksgiving Day and Shaun's birthday---we miss the whole day of November 23!

——— ——— ———

The flight reservations using air miles for this trip were made nine months ago and, much to Linda's chagrin, I made them for coach class. She has been in a constant state of panic about that ever since. And now, as I am sitting on the plane preparing to push back from the gate at SeaTac, she is working with the flight attendants to get our seats reassigned!

After making the international flight reservations to and from Hanoi, I went to work planning the details of our travel through Vietnam and Laos. I talked with several people who had traveled Vietnam and read three guide books, cover to cover, a Vietnamese history book and *The Quiet American*, a novel set in Vietnam during the 1960's. I developed a pretty good sense of what I wanted to see.

Roger Winters, one of our investors who had bicycled through Vietnam last year, supplied me with the names of the guides he used. That resulted in me contacting several of them as well as a tour agency. Only Vietnamese citizens can drive in Vietnam, so we needed drivers, hopefully English-speaking. I emailed several of them but then found out that the tour agency, BA Tours, was willing to find all my drivers as well as to make all my hotel reservations and flight reservations. That is no surprise, after all, that is what travel agencies do. But having BA Tours do all the work would only cost us maybe $500 more for the whole month of travel! Done deal! Only $7,600 US for both of us for hotels, air, car, driver, guides, most breakfasts and lunches and entrance fees where required---in both Vietnam and Laos. Pretty impressive. I can't imagine how many hours I saved myself by having BA Tours do all of the reserving and arranging.

We are leaving Seattle toward the end of one of the rainiest months ever recorded in Seattle. In fact, if two more inches fall in the next nine days, it will be the rainiest ever

(15 inches or so for the month). As I sit here on the plane on the tarmac at SeaTac, it is raining.

We had a comfortable start to our day. Britt gave us a ride at 9 a.m. from our house to the airport so we could arrive 3½ hours before our flight. This is the busiest travel day of the year and we are leaving in the middle of it. Naturally, as these things go, we got checked in and through security in only fifteen minutes! Oh well, we moved on to the Admiral's Club and I did something I never do---I had a Bloody Mary! We also had someone take our picture to launch our photo book.

I need to spend some of this flight reading about Seoul. Linda made all the plans for the one-day lay-over we have there, so I need to get caught up. As I said earlier, we should get to our hotel in Seoul around midnight on the 23rd and we will depart Seoul bound for Hanoi around 7:30 p.m. on the 24th, so we will have a full day to knock around the city. Hopefully, we will be able to get 6 to 7 hours of sleep after our midnight arrival and then we are thinking we will take a bus tour of Seoul that morning. The one-day Seoul lay-over should have the added benefit of allowing us more time to adjust to the time zone changes. Hanoi is only two hours different than Seoul (Hanoi is fifteen hours ahead of Seattle time).

——— ——— ———

Okay, now I am an expert on Seoul. At least I know where it is on the map, the currency and how to get from the airport at Incheon to our hotel in Seoul. It should take a little more than an hour and cost around $50 US (50,000 won). And, I learned Koreans do not expect tips. I know it all; we are covered.

We've now been in the air around four hours and are flying over the southern coast of Alaska. We've been doing so for an hour and the shoreline is incredible; pretty stark looking, no trees---and I mean, not one---in this part of Alaska. We are flying over the "hip and thigh" of the Aleutian chain, Kodiak Island, Salmon Bay, Dillingham and places with names ending in ak, uk, ik and ok! We have gone from rugged, endless snow-capped volcanic mountains to flat, pot-holed, icy, barren land. Now we will head out to sea again, north of the Aleutian peninsula. We will later cross the very western tip of the Aleutian chain heading south at the international date line over the Kamchatka Peninsula of Russia and then on to Tokyo. Since we are following the sun as we head west (generally), it will be light this entire flight to Tokyo. It will be dark, though, during our flight from Tokyo to Seoul.

As a result of her friendly haggling session with the flight attendants, Linda was able to secure a bulkhead seat, but I was unwilling to give up my window seat, so she is sitting a couple of rows ahead of me in the middle row of seats at a bulkhead. There is no question about what she is doing; her occasional, rather loud outbursts of laughter indicate she is enjoying her movie. Hopefully, the movie won't turn sad or we all will be listening to her bawling! Oh God, now she is laughing and clapping! Since it is an on-demand movie, no one will be watching the same movie at the same time so everyone will simply assume she is looney. It's okay. Sitting back here I can pretend I don't know her. I am going to keep my head down; read some more about Korean history.

——— ——— ———

After ten hours in the air, we just landed at the Narita Airport in Japan. It is 11 p.m. Seattle time; it is 4 p.m. the next day in Japan. We have a couple-hour lay-over here before continuing on to Seoul.

We are sitting in Northwest Airline's Admiral's Club at Narita. Even though we will be departing on the same plane in an hour for Seoul, we had to grab all of our belongings, deplane and go through a passport and security screening. We then circled around to a gate that led us back to the same airplane. I don't really understand that process, but there must be a reason.

In any event, we ended up in the Admiral's Club where we discovered the coolest beer dispenser ever! You take a chilled beer glass, set it on the machine and push a button. The machine tips the glass, pours beer down the side of the glass almost to the top, stops, rights the glass and then tops it off with beer foam. Pretty damn cool. Linda took a picture of me getting a beer from it.

I strolled through the Narita airport a little trying to get a feel for it. It was built fairly recently and is supposed to be a modern marvel of sorts, but it is hard to get a sense of that from what I can see in the international area. It is also supposed to be on an island, but it clearly isn't (unless they are talking about the huge island of Honshu!). On our approach into the airport on the plane, we flew over farmlands and villages for twenty miles after dropping below the clouds and before landing. I will have to Google it when I get home; see what I am missing.

FRIDAY, NOVEMBER 24

Linda crosses a street in Seoul

It is 9 a.m. in Seoul, 4 p.m. Thanksgiving Day in Seattle, a day earlier. I am at our hotel in Seoul having coffee.

Our arrival at Incheon airport at 9 p.m. last night was uneventful. The big, beautiful airport had our luggage out in no time, immigration and customs were hardly slow-downs in our walk toward the airport exit. I had calculated how much won we needed to get through our one day here and exchanged $150 US for 135,000 won. A taxi cab driver greeted us as we walked out of the airport offering to get us to Seoul. Will I ever get to a foreign city and not have a taxi cab story? Even I am getting tired of them! Here goes:

First of all, the guide book made no mention of issues with cabs from Incheon to Seoul and implied all metered cabs were regulated and okay to use. I asked the driver how much it would cost to get to Seoul before we got into the car and he gave me the only English word he (pretended) to know: "meter". I even asked a second time, but learned his English hadn't expanded in the five minutes that had passed. Oh well, the guide books had given me no reason for concern and it was the equivalent of 4 a.m. my time; I was a little rummy.

I make note when the driver trips the meter that it starts out at 4,500 won, just like the guide book said it is supposed to. I look to see if he has the meter set at the correct tariff, but see no indicator on the meter. The guide books indicate that without traffic, the ride into Seoul should cost around 50,000 won. I start sensing some trouble when moving along at 70 to 80 mph one-quarter of the way to Seoul and the meter is already at 25,000 won! I am tired, I lay my head back comforted in the knowledge that the driver can't take me for more than the 135,000 won I have in my pocket!

At the hotel, I get out of the car, start gathering our luggage and reaching for my wallet all while also trying to get my reading glasses on so I can read the piece of paper the driver is waving at me. He had pulled an invoice out of the glove compartment. It read 100,000 won; the meter reads 86,000 won! I shake my head "No" to the 100,000 won invoice and say the one English word I have in common with this scoundrel: "meter". About this time the driver spies the porter from the hotel coming up to our car. In response, the driver turns and quickly reaches inside the car and prints a receipt out from the meter. Mostly ignoring him, his new receipt and his nervousness over the porter's presence, I count out 85,000 won and shove it into his hand; he, in turn, makes sure to hand me the newly printed receipt, hops in his taxi and drives away.

The porter, learning what had just happened was upset (on my behalf) that I had paid so much. This morning, in better light, I can see the printed receipt from the meter says 59,000 won---probably the legitimate amount. I don't know what he did to get his meter to display 86,000 won, but then to print 59,000 won, but clearly it was the fare he wanted the porter to see if he was questioned. Clearly, his gimmick has worked for him before, probably many times.

Anyway, no matter how I might try, I can't seem to avoid issues with taxis from international airports!

Time to go explore Seoul.

——— ——— ———

We are about to board our Korean Air flight to Hanoi. We are sitting at the Incheon Airport---one of the nicest in which we have ever been. We have a 7:30 p.m. departure and a five-hour flight. We lose two hours and get into Hanoi at 10:30 p.m. Hopefully, the private driver we have arranged for through BA Tours will be there to greet us (I will miss the opportunity for another aggravating taxi cab ride from an international airport). I was able to email BA Tours from the Admiral's Club in Seoul about an hour ago to confirm our driver, so we should be okay.

We had a non-eventful, pre-negotiated, fixed-price taxi ride to the Incheon airport from our hotel, getting to the airport around 4 p.m. Checking into our flight was simple and organized.

Seoul is a great city! We hopped on a tour bus this morning, as planned, but found it to be more about transportation than tourism. It did give us a good windshield view of the north side of the Han River. We saw a very modern city, and a very Western one. The city for most practical purposes has

been re-built since the end of the Korean War in the late 1950's. Much of the reconstruction occurred in the mid-1970's and then again later in preparation for the 1988 Olympic Summer games, which apparently did a lot for the city. We were admittedly in the city's main financial area and the area where the major palaces are, but I was impressed with how clean Seoul is; clean, organized and well-maintained.

As we rode along on our bus tour, we decided it was not doing for us what we wanted and debated where to get off and what to do after we did. Our choice was to get off at Insa-dong, a small, compact neighborhood (or "dong") and is one of the few areas of Seoul to have maintained its past character; narrow alleyways with quaint cafes and shops---a cool place.

We had spent ninety minutes on the bus and an hour in Insa-dong before walking up to the Gyeonbokgung Palace where we watched the changing of the guard. The changing of the guard is a long, slow process dating back to the Joseon Dynasty in the 16th century. We walked back to the hotel at about 1:00 p.m. to freshen up. We left again to walk down the street with the Cheonggyecheon Stream running down its middle. It is a business district street with high-rise buildings and the stream with a nice walkway alongside. It was a nice place.

Linda spied a traditional-looking Korean restaurant in an alleyway so we stopped in for some food. Thank God for a Korean couple sitting nearby who spoke English! With their help we ordered a simple authentic Korean lunch. We were warned that the soup may be too spicy for us; it was pretty spicy, but very good. There were a couple of things we did not finish eating because they were just too spicy, but it was all very good, and lots of fun.

I just used an airport computer to send this group email home:

> ***SEOUL, SOUTH KOREA***
> ***Subject: In Seoul***
>
> *Hey everyone! We just spent a busy, but great, day exploring Seoul and leave in about an hour for Hanoi. It is 6 pm on the 24th in Seoul (about 1 am on the 24th for you). We will get into Hanoi about 10:30 pm tonight, about 7:30 am for you all.*
>
> *This damn computer at the Northwest Airlines club room is all in Korean! I can't figure out how to use my "Travel List" to mail everyone---you represent the few emails I can remember. But just wanted to write and let you know we are safe and having fun. Britt, could I bother you to look up my sister's email on the list of names I gave you and forward this to her. It is Sheila Jensen, she will let my Mother, other sister and brother know we have reported in. Thank you.*
>
> *Ok....know if I can figure out which of these buttons is "Send".....*
>
> *Gary*

——— ——— ———

We are currently 35,000 feet over somewhere three hours south of Seoul in a Korean Airline's Airbus 300-600. This is a true cattle car flight. This wide-body, two-aisle plane has only three rows of first class seats and all the rest of the plane is economy, in only one cabin, so you can see the whole length of the plane. Pretty unusual. And since I can see everyone on the flight, I can accurately report that we are one of two Caucasian couples on board. My gray hair and Linda's blonde look like beacons, not to mention my height. When I stood up a minute ago to look to the back of the plane, everyone looked at me. Makes me feel like a monkey in a zoo; guess I'll stay seated.

It was a short but pleasant stay in Seoul. We found Koreans to be very friendly, outwardly and openly helpful, clean, well-dressed and attractive. All-in-all, Seoul was a great experience for us. Hopefully, the one-day lay-over will help with our jet lag so that we can hit the ground running in Vietnam!

SATURDAY, NOVEMBER 25

Our hotel in Hanoi, the Hoa Binh Hotel

After eighteen hours with my butt in an airplane seat, we are finally in Hanoi. It is 8 a.m. and I am sitting in the breakfast room of the Hoa Binh Hotel in or near the Old Quarter of Hanoi.

Our five-hour flight from Seoul last night landed a little later than scheduled, at 10:40 p.m. During the entire flight the plane was hot and stuffy so we weren't very excited to deplane into a very crowded, low-ceilinged, hot and muggy immigration area. Gary stood in line for over an hour; Gary was hot and tired; Gary was ready for cool and sleep. Gary was among the very last to get through immigration. Others had been much cleverer than Gary about changing lines to find faster moving ones.

When we finally got through immigration we walked into a mostly empty baggage area to see that there were no bags on the carousel! It was then about 11:45 p.m. (almost 2 a.m. Seoul time) and I could not find our baggage claim checks so we could find an airline agent to start the search for our missing luggage. I think the portion of the ticket with the claim checks was torn off by the boarding agent in Seoul. My exhausted, jet-lagged mind is starting to process what the next dreadful steps were going to have to be when I suddenly see Linda's bag fall onto the carousel, followed shortly by mine. No bag of any kind had come onto the carousel for over fifteen minutes and now our two, and only our two, drop onto it! How can that be? I decided I didn't need to know and I surely didn't care. We gratefully grabbed our bags and trudged past the customs inspector who did nothing but give us a simple nod; wanted to be home as badly as we did. Not an auspicious start to a month of travel through Vietnam!

We immediately spied the "Gary Brown and Linda Griffin" placard being held by a pixie-cute Vietnamese girl, our guide. We had never before walked out of an airport to be greeted by a guide and it bothered me to be one of those "coddled" travelers. But I got over it. It was a very nice relief after what had been a less-than-perfect arrival. She walked us outside where a car was waiting with a male driver. It was a 45-minute drive to the hotel during which there was little conversation; it was by then 1 a.m. (3 a.m. Seoul time). We were exhausted.

I am sure our guide and driver were, too. Even though they are accustomed to picking up arrivals, I am sure, Linda and I had to be at least thirty minutes later than everyone else on our plane in getting out of the airport. I suspect they had been waiting for well over an hour without even knowing that we were on the plane. We are lucky they were still there. We will get to know her, who speaks reasonably good English, and him, who didn't speak last night, much better over the next week as we will be spending a lot of time with them.

Linda had been hot, tired and menstrual since boarding the plane in Seoul. Gary was hot, tired and fed up with menopause by the time we got to our hotel room. We tried splitting a cold beer from our hotel room's icebox to relax us and put us in better moods, but quickly realized the only way we were going to get along was by going to sleep!

With that in mind and anxious to get a good night's sleep, I took an Ambien---my God, do those work well! Judging from the way my reading glasses and guide book were strewn about the floor when I got out of bed this morning, I must have literally fallen asleep before laying down. I only got six hours of sleep, but they were good ones!

Today is a "free" day. We won't see our guide and driver again until tomorrow morning. I will use the day to get oriented and see some things that we aren't slated to see with our guide. I need to get some dong: 16,000 dong per US dollar. I will have a handful.

——— ——— ———

Wow! Mindboggling. It is actually indescribable. The motorcycles and scooters in this city. We have all seen the pictures, but I am here to tell you, nothing short of standing on a street corner and witnessing it can ever come close to giving one a true idea of what I am talking about. Everyone---and everything---moves on a scooter or motorcycle. The streets are gutter to gutter filled with them. The drivers are skillful; seemingly unaffected by the mass of scooters inches from their own, cutting in front of them, whizzing by them. Drivers are totally unemotional and uncaring; the constant horn beeping is contrary to the calm and ease they all seem to exude as they marshal their two-wheeled transport through the maze. They talk with each other as they motor side-by-side, talk on cell phones; they even text as they drive, calmly looking around, never

evincing any anxiety, even as they cross through a five-street intersection with no traffic lights or controls. It is just absolutely amazing to watch---I could do so for hours!

——— ——— ———

I had been writing at a street side café in the Old Quarter of Hanoi when I suddenly realized it was time to get back to the hotel and shower for my massage. I hailed a "Xe Om" (motorcycle taxi) and offered 10,000 dong for the fifteen block ride to the Hoa Binh Hotel; that is 60 cents US. That was my first Xe Om ride and it won't be my last since it is about the only way to get around without walking. I got a chuckle from the other Xe Om drivers as I got on this little scooter that was being driven by an average-size (meaning small) Vietnamese guy. I must look huge on the back of those little machines!

——— ——— ———

Post massage…aaahh!

Let me back up to this morning. After Linda and I ate some breakfast at our hotel, we took off on foot to explore. We first stopped and got 3,200,000 dong ($200 US), but the whole time walking the few blocks to exchange cash, we were agog at the street scene. But then, I already wrote about that. It isn't just the cycles in the streets, it's the shops, the people; the hustle and bustle of activity. People jostling, hurrying, but never unfriendly or pushy. These people have learned how to live in close quarters without attitude; it's refreshing. Even the constant horn honking seems friendly, and as Linda says, it does seem to be more in warning than aggression.

The Old Quarter through which we walked and spent the entire day, started 1,000 years ago when the streets were canals. Thirty-six different guilds each had their own street (canal) and the street was named after their trade, or "hang". To this day the streets are named Hang Gia, for the silk trade, Hang something-else for plumbing and another Hang for stationery. Today, Linda and I walked through Hangs for shoes, books, for booze and for beds, among several others.

Due to the old tax laws which assessed taxes based on how much sidewalk (or canal) space your building took up, all the buildings are very narrow, maybe 6 to 8 feet, and very deep. And since no one dared build higher than the King's palace, all the buildings are two stories or less.

I have decided Vietnamese are not small by genetics, I think it came from necessity! It is amazing how many Vietnamese you will see squatting in one of the tiny, narrow shops eating or working. It is also common, if not without exception, for these activities

to spill over onto the sidewalk in front of their narrow building, making it necessary to step over, around and through people as you navigate your way down any

sidewalk. We would step between scores of people who were eating lunch while squatting on the sidewalk in front of the little café that served them. And, of course, motorcycles are parked everywhere and usually on the already limited sidewalk. Although I did see one elegant and expensive-looking shop where the owners' three motorcycles were parked inside the store in front of the artwork that was for sale; remember the store was eight feet wide, at most!

Can you (whoever you are) read this? I am sitting next door to our hotel at a street-side café having a beer waiting for Linda at about 7 p.m., and it is dark and I can't really see! So, quit complaining about my handwriting!

SUNDAY, NOVEMBER 26

Hanoi's Old Quarter

I am sitting in our Hanoi hotel's breakfast room, having coffee and allowing Linda time to get ready for the day. She will join me soon for breakfast. Let me go back to yesterday to describe our day in more detail.

Linda and I walked the streets and alleyways of Old Quarter for several hours yesterday, seeing more of the same thing and never getting tired of it. We walked through the huge three-story indoor Dong Xuan market which was jammed pack with stalls offering nonfood items. The guide book says the market employs 3,000 people.

We sat down at a main intersection to rest our weary legs, cool down and get something to drink, after a foggy but muggy morning. The sun had come out and it was simply down-right hot. We sipped cokes and watched in amazement as people, cycles, buses and cars negotiated their way through the unregulated intersection in front of us. Afterward, we walked down the silk street where Linda wanted to do some shopping. I didn't last that long with that so we agreed to meet back at the hotel.

After making sure Linda had a map and knew where the Hoa Binh Hotel was, I took off for more walking and gawking---for about an hour-and-a-half. I walked by the Hanoi Opera House which is near out hotel. I took advantage of the proximity to my hotel room and went to it rest my feet and cool down while I re-read portions of the guide book. Then, I headed back out to see some areas I had missed. It was about an hour later, around 4:30 p.m., that I was sitting at the street side café when I realized I had to get back to the hotel for my massage and hopped the Xe Om, the motorcycle taxi.

When I got back to the hotel from my Xe Om ride, Linda had left me a note saying she was getting a massage, herself. I showered quickly and then went out to get my massage: $7.50 US for a ninety minute massage. As weary as my feet and back were, any rubbing by a cute Vietnamese girl was going to be appreciated, and it was, but frankly, the massage wasn't that good. At one point she seemed to get infatuated with my right thigh. I was about to ask her to move on to another part of my body before she rubbed the skin off my thigh, when she finally moved on. Linda and I both discovered, too late, that when massages are that inexpensive, the expectation is you tip them 100%, or equal to the amount charged. Linda's masseuse wasn't very happy with her. I was afraid mine would go after my right thigh again, so I just left some money and got outta there!

After I showered again after my massage, Linda and I met at the café next door to our hotel where I was writing in the dark in my journal. We left there and went into the Old Quarter for dinner at a place I had seen earlier. Linda would not take a Xe Om so we hailed a cyclo, a three-wheeled pedal cycle with a two-person carriage in front. My fat ass and Linda's little one barely fit. These guys aren't used to moving men my size around. I agreed to pay him 50,000 dong ($3 US) and he pedaled (getting off and pushing us on busy streets) for ten minutes to get us to our destination. He acted exhausted, so I gave him a 10,000 dong tip (generous, aren't I?). We asked a Xe Om driver sitting alongside the street in front of our café to take our picture in the cyclo.

The restaurant was called "La" and is owned by a Canadian from Vancouver. Expensive by Vietnam standards, it was a good place to eat in a cool, clean atmosphere. From there we walked to a little bar, had a drink and chatted with a young Vietnamese woman owner who learned her very good English sitting behind her bar. Linda was still unwilling to take a Xe Om, so we walked most all the way back to the hotel. As we neared the hotel, Linda took her shoes off because they were bothering her. She walked about two blocks barefoot before a cyclo happened by to take us the last few blocks.

It had been a long, but awesome, first day in Vietnam.

Linda has joined me in the hotel's breakfast room and we are having breakfast. Our guide will meet us at 9:30 a.m. for a day of touring. We will see things today we didn't see yesterday. One of which is the Ho Chi Minh mausoleum. The guy's body is kept on display, like the Russians do with Lenin and did with Stalin (who was later buried). Visitors to the mausoleum have to wear long pants, so I am sitting here sweltering in jeans. I think I will take a pair of shorts along with us so I can put them on when we are finished with Ho Chi Minh; it is way too hot for jeans! The fog has already burned off. It will be a hot day.

——— ——— ———

Okay, that was a full day of sight-seeing! It is 7 p.m. and I am sitting in the same place having a beer next to our hotel in the same bad light writing as I was last night. Linda is getting ready so she and I can go have dinner.

We started our day by going by Uncle Ho's house (mausoleum) and seeing him in all his dead glory. Vietnamese revere him, as perhaps they should. But frankly it is a little hard to determine if they really revere him or are just afraid not to. When we got to the mausoleum we had to buy a shirt for Linda because her shoulders were showing; that is not allowed. I don't have much to say about good ol' Ho except that he is dead; quite clearly so. We also saw the Presidential Palace and the much more humble homes Ho lived in while running his country and the wars against it. First, the French and then the Americans.

Huang, our petite (maybe 4'10', but more likely 4'9") guide is a bundle of information. She has Vietnam history down pat and, strangely, it's the same history as reported in the guide books, so I was able to follow along. Her English is good, but the pronunciation, especially of place names, is difficult unless you know the things she is talking about.

After the mausoleum, we drove a short distance (we were still in the Ba Dinh area of Hanoi) to the Temple of Literature and then to the Fine Arts Museum. These were a wee bit esoteric for us, but they are on every guide book's "must see" list. At the museum, we sat outside and had tea/coke with Huang and another guide that works for the same company as Huang. We decided we should have Pho for lunch. Pho is the Vietnamese rice noodle soup. Huang took us to the perfect place and gave us some clues as to how to mix things together for the Pho. I am glad I heeded her warning about the Chile paste---a little dab does indeed go a long ways! It turns out northern Vietnamese cuisine is not spicy, that is mostly the province of southern cuisine. Chile paste, however, is hot of course no matter at what latitude you happen to be. The food was great and it was a fairly quick lunch. We didn't get started with lunch until after 1 p.m. and were on the road in the car again before 2 p.m.; on the road to the Vietnam Military Museum.

The Vietnam Military Museum. It is a wee bit difficult walking through the trophy case of the team who whipped your team. I actually experienced a little pang when I saw the Vietnamese fighter jet in front of the museum with a dozen small American flags on its nose denoting the fighter pilot's success in shooting down U.S. pilots. I understand, though, they have toned down considerably the anti-American sentiment in the museum's displays (not good for the American tourism dollar). But really, it seemed from reading what they have changed was, and what remains still is, less about anti-anything and more about "Yay for our side", which if you care to notice, is exactly what American museums and memorials are all about.

I understand some of the displays were very recently changed. The removal, for example, of the display in the museum's American War section of the Ford Edsel crashed through a wall to signify "another great American flop". This and other recent changes were made in preparation for the APEC (Asian Pacific Economic Council) meetings that were held here in Hanoi just last week. President George W. Bush was here for that. The APEC meetings were a real opportunity for Hanoi to showcase itself and they didn't want and Edsel screwing things up for them.

It wasn't until after we had left the museum that I realized I hadn't taken any pictures inside the museum. Like I said, being there wasn't that easy.

We left the military museum about 3 p.m. and were dropped off with Huang in the Old Quarter near where we were scheduled to see the Water Puppet show at 4 p.m. the three of us went shopping on the "shoe street" for some cheap shoes for Linda to wear trekking in Sapa over the next few days.

That mission accomplished we walked through a nearby food market. Food markets in Asia are always interesting---not for the weak stomach---and this one was no exception. I was surprised we didn't lose Linda when Huang pointed out the skinned, cooked dog. And I was even more impressed when Linda failed to maul Huang when she admitted to having eaten dog meat, even though she owns four (used to be five....kidding!). We watched a lady merchant reaching into a bag of live frogs, making her selection, handing the live little critter to the vendor who promptly chopped off its head before cutting the legs off for the customer. Dinner anyone?

The hour-long Water Puppet show was just okay. It is a 1,000 year tradition, not known outside North Vietnam until fifty years ago and was truly a must-see; I am glad though it wasn't any longer than it was.

And then the five-star part of the day: Huang took us to a massage place---a top-end place at $10 US per hour. Other than having to walk up three narrow flights of stairs, it was the best massage I have had in a long time. We went from under-tipping for massages last night to over-tipping today. The manager of the massage place followed me into the street trying to return some of my money, but I insisted he split the excess between the two girls who massaged us. They were delighted; he was indifferent.

TUESDAY, NOVEMBER 28

Bucolic scene along the drive from Hanoi to Sapa

Yesterday was brutal. We left Hanoi at 7 a.m. and arrived at the Hotel Victoria in Sapa at 7 p.m. last night. Sapa is a mountain village in northwest Vietnam, very near the China border.

At something more than 400 kilometers, it was a long drive, but the killer was the very rough, winding road we traveled. It was paved the whole way, but only wide enough for cars to pass by each other with their outside wheels in the gravel on the road's shoulder. I handled sitting in the back seat with Linda for the first eight hours, but then, knowing I wasn't doing all that well with the motion, the driver and Huang started feeling sorry for me and insisted I get in the front seat; which I did for the last four hours of the journey. It helped, but it was too late, I was saddled with that awful motion sickness feeling until I went to sleep that night.

The long car ride was interesting and, provided we can avoid the same drive returning to Hanoi, worth it---believe it or not!

Pulling away yesterday morning from our Hanoi hotel on a busy Monday morning, we saw Hanoi traffic at it's, uh, best? I remember writing pages in my journal in Cambodia about the way drivers casually drive into oncoming traffic to initiate a turn to the left side of the road, whether or not at an intersection. The same thing occurs in Hanoi, times 1,000!---many, many more people and vehicles. It is just incredible to watch a motorcyclist simply turn left into an oncoming wall of other motorcycles, cars, buses and trucks, moving across the oncoming lane as that traffic accommodatingly parts to let him through. It is something you have to witness to really understand, not that I do!

It doesn't all work perfectly here in the unregulated traffic world of Vietnam, however. Our driver pulled around a downed motorcycle in the middle of a Hanoi street on which an older woman and a young boy had apparently been riding. Seemingly unhurt, she was gathering her strewn belongings and trying to right the cycle as the boy stood by and the traffic zoomed past them. On the highway an hour north of Hanoi where traffic was lighter but moving along faster at 30 to 40 mph, the consequences of a collision are a little more dire. The accident aftermath we witnessed had two motorcycles in pieces with a sandal sitting in a pretty large pool of blood. Even that far out of Hanoi, the volume of traffic, 90% of which is motorcycles, is still staggering. How closely they maneuver to each other and how they so casually walk or drive into oncoming traffic boggles the Westerner's mind.

In the rural areas, the highway is every community's lifeline and almost becomes a social center. Kids sit on the road's edge playing a game as cars and trucks zoom by just feet away; dogs dart into the road; oxen lumber slowly

across, kids bicycle to and from school in the middle of the road, even at night without lights. On rural roads we averaged 20 to 25 mph for hours mostly because of how rough the roadway was. It was not a comfortable ride. We stopped every couple of hours including 45 minutes for a lunch break.

In this thin sliver of a country, there are 84,000,000 people, so there aren't many uninhabited areas. But we did see pristine and pastoral countryside during our drive. We got to Lao Cai just before dark. Lao Cai is the border town where you can cross the Red River and enter China. This has only been possible since 2001 when the two countries kissed and made up for past differences. We took pictures of us with China in the background and then watched a Shaman do some sort of

ritual for her followers. Not sure I understood it all, but it is some practice of ancestor worship and animism.

Our guide, Huang, is a walking website; she has her stuff down pat. I have read enough to know she knows her stuff accurately, but I'll bet she is a bore to her friends. She can quote exchange rates in scores of currencies. She has her country's history to its geological formation down to the year and understands her country's current economic challenges and functioning. She relates the cultural history of the tribal communities we are seeing with precision (I know because I have checked her against the guide books). She is very efficient and on-the-spot with her guide responsibilities and organization. She has taught herself English and some Mandarin. She can't be any older than 25. And, she was probably class president and made fun of by her peers.

Linda and I were very road-weary when we checked into the Victoria Hotel in Sapa last night. And, as I mentioned, I was feeling pretty "punk" from motion sickness. We

cleaned up a little in our hotel room and then went to the cozy lounge in the hotel and sat by the fireplace which was burning real wood. Sapa is a mountain village and it is cool here, probably about 45 degrees last night. We had beer and wine and played a solitaire game that was quick, so I would play it, and easy, so I could.

We also chatted with some travelers from Belgium and another couple; he was from England and we think she might have been a local escort. She was very cute and sexy and in a short, short skirt. If she was his wife, he did good! If an escort, he did good---and smart! He (and maybe her, we couldn't quite figure that out) had also driven in from Hanoi and had also just arrived. But his ride was delayed because his driver fell asleep and wrecked the car! No one got hurt. This was not a good thing for me to hear, because I was very concerned with our driver, Hung, during the last hour of our drive as we climbed up the mountainside on the narrow mountain road between Lao Cai and Sapa. It was, by then, dark and he was clearly groggy. I almost grabbed the steering wheel at one point. Hearing the Englishman's story I am glad I was in the front seat!

Linda and I ate dinner here at our hotel; it was a good meal, not great, but it didn't matter because it was easy and comfortable and that was what we needed. I do not remember my head hitting the pillow. It had been a long, long day.

I was up, showered and downstairs on the lobby computer by 7:00 this morning. I wanted to get an email out to everyone so my mother would know we are okay. I did get a quick email out in South Korea, but was unable to access my travel distribution list, so that email was just sent to Jaret, Chuck, Dennis and Britt, who I asked to email my sisters so they could, in turn, convey the message to mom. But, I apparently failed to enter Britt's email address because it bounced back. Anyway, this morning's email seemed to go out to everyone:

SAPA, VIETNAM
Subject: Greetings from Vietnam

Hello all.... I sent an earlier message to some of you (whose emails I could remember) from Seoul.... I had trouble getting my distribution list to work in Korean.

We are in day 4 or so of our trip...two days in Hanoi and a day traveling to where we are....tsunami safe Sapa.....6,600 feet above sea level in the mountains of Vietnam very near the China border. We had a tortuous 12-hour trip by car yesterday getting here, but saw some beautiful country and lots of rice fields and water buffalo. As one might expect, it is an amazing country....there will be stories to tell.

Today we are trekking through the rice fields in the mountains to visit one of the tribal villages. It will be a long day, but anything is better than that friggin' car!

Having lots of fun...and managed to escape the plane journey free of colds and other illnesses...so feeling well (the daily $7 massage helps!). Computers aren't plentiful so not sure how often I will be able to write.

Hope all is well with everyone.

Gary

I have been sitting having coffee and breakfast while writing in my journal. It is time now for Linda and me to hook up with Huang for our day's adventures.

WEDNESDAY, NOVEMBER 29

Terraced rice fields near Sapa

Yesterday, we met up with Huang and Hung at about 9 a.m. and drove out of the small town of Sapa for about ninety minutes along a steep cliff overlooking a large valley below. We stopped along the sliver of a road several times to take pictures of the terraced rice fields---just like what you see in the postcards. Actually, since the fields are between crops, they aren't as colorful as at other times of the year, so I would like to find a good postcard, or maybe a painting of the terraced fields.

As we drove along we were seeing members of both the Black Hmong and Red Zao tribes; mostly all women and children dressed in their colorful garb, and most of whom were trying to sell their woven hats, scarves and blankets. I rolled the window down and gave one child Hmong girl 2,000 dong for a little trinket.

About ¼ of the way down the side of the valley, Linda, Huang and I got out of the car and started the two-plus hour walk down into and along the valley floor following a dirt road/trail. At one point we stopped at a hut occupied by several women and children, a pig or two, and two cute, cuddly little dogs (guess where Linda's attention went). We were allowed into the hut; a dirt floored, very low ceiling, three-room affair. It was pretty humbling to see the conditions in which they were living. I took a picture after asking permission and then gave them 20,000 dong ($.60 US) as we left.

We also stopped at a government-funded school perched on the hillside. Again, a pretty humble affair. Kids were either in the class room flicking through the pages of their text books or in the small dirt yard playing. It was an elementary school. The kids were very cute.

It is not a busy time of year in the rice fields for these tribes since they are in their winter and between crops. The men apparently go away into the mountains for a prolonged period of time this time of year to hunt and collect bark (for incense), which explains why weren't seeing any. If it were a busy time of year, kids would not have been in school; education is not valued by the tribes and the kids would be needed in the fields.

It was a great day for the walk, dry, not windy with blue sky and pretty warm, maybe 80 degrees. We walked

through a couple of different villages and saw a third tribe called Tsay (I have seen several different spellings) who are shyer and wear colorful plaid headdresses. It is apparently this tribe with whom most of the tourist home stays occur. Huang says, even though shyer, they are cleaner than the Hmong or Zao.

We stopped at a little store in the village to use the restroom and buy water. Two Red Zao women approached me to sell me a woven hat. The Red Zao women shave their eyebrows and a portion of their hairline and wear

bright red headdresses. They tie their hair in a topknot to which they tie the red turban. As I sat in the chair waiting for Linda to finish in the restroom, the Red Zao woman put one of their hats on my head. I had Huang take my picture with the hat on and with the Red Zao woman. I gave the woman a US dollar bill for the photograph with her (which delighted her) and we walked on. After taking a few wrong turns, we found our way to the bridge to cross the river where Hung was waiting for us in the car.

When we got into the car with Huang this morning, we informed her we were changing plans. Linda and I would be taking the night train back to Hanoi; no offense, Huang, but we have no interest in repeating the torturous car journey back into Hanoi. The only space available on the train was, of course, the most expensive, $100 US each, but it is a private cabin and we will save the cost of the hotel room. The train leaves Lao Cai at 9 p.m. and arrives in Hanoi around 6 a.m. the next morning. We will have an hour bus ride to get from Sapa to Lao Cai. With that change, Huang and Hung dropped us off at the Hotel Victoria after our morning trek about 1 p.m. They left immediately to start their drive back to Hanoi; they will get there around midnight (if Hung stays awake!) When I made this sound like such a hardship for them, they just shrugged their shoulders; we must seem like such wimps to them.

Linda and I had the rest of the afternoon to ourselves. We walked the town of Sapa. I walked through the market and exchanged cash while Linda had some pizza for lunch. I just wasn't hungry. I had a ninety-minute massage around 4 p.m. It was a pretty relaxed afternoon.

The spa at the nearby hotel where I had my massage is, like most of them, open; that is, the massage rooms have curtains and the walls don't reach the ceiling, so you can easily hear conversations in nearby rooms. Toward the end of my massage, we heard voices and footsteps as someone approached the neighboring room for a massage. It became apparent that it was an English-speaking couple who were about to get massages at the same time in the same room. The attendant had shown them their room and then left. I hear the woman's voice: "What do we do? Get naked? Do we leave our underwear on? Well, I guess no one is here to tell us, so we should just get naked and cover up with a towel." He isn't saying anything and she is nervously jabbering and tittering. It was so funny to me because Linda and I had been in the same predicament in Bali in 2000. I hear rustling of clothes and more tittering, "Oh my, honey, we aren't in Minnesota anymore!" Damn, I had trouble containing myself! It turns out, Linda had earlier talked to a couple from Minnesota. There can't be many from Minnesota in this small, isolated mountain village, so it has to be the same couple. I hope we see them so Linda can point them out to me. I would love to put faces to that conversation.

After our lazy afternoon, Linda and I showered and went down to the fireplace in the lobby of our hotel. We started talking with Amanda and Melinda from Australia. We had a pretty raucous time with them and ended up eating dinner with them. Two mid-thirties, married mothers with kids and husbands at home. The two ladies were taking a nine-day holiday by themselves. We had lots of yuks about kids, spouses and everything else, getting louder and more animated with every glass of wine. Then we started "naked" stories, starting with my sharing the Minnesota couple's story, but everyone had more stories to share. Melinda told about how she grabbed her suitcase in the lobby of their Hanoi hotel and swung it around to put it onto a cart not realizing the suitcase was not zipped closed. Her clothes ended up all over the lobby floor. She was appalled at the male valets picking up her bras and dirty underwear. A funny story made better by the Australian accents. God, we laughed a lot!

After dinner we four walked to our fireplace seats in the lobby where a couple from London was sitting. They joined in on our fun until midnight when we all finally went to our rooms. We made a date to join up again at 5 p.m. this afternoon before Linda and I catch the bus to Lao Cai.

The London couple was actually a Belgian man and a Vietnamese woman, but she was born and raised in Belgium; this was her second visit to Vietnam. They were both commodities traders working in London and had been dating for six years. He is 32, she is 36. Both were very bright and fun; my guess is she is really sharp and makes very good money.

I just checked emails. There is 5 inches of snow in Seattle! Glad we are here.

——— ——— ———

We took off from the hotel about 10 a.m. this morning to walk to the village of Cat Cat, about three kilometers away. It is down the hill from Sapa in the opposite direction we went with Huang yesterday. It sure seemed like more than three kilometers, we seemed to go downhill forever. It was a fun walk, but was less interesting than yesterday's. It was, though, beautiful weather and fairly easy walking. Thank God there were Xe Oms at the bottom of the hill; it would have been a steep trek back up. It was only the unattractive prospect of walking back up the steep hill that got Linda on the back of a Xe Om. She hung on to that dude for dear life---it was pretty funny.

We have an interesting night and day ahead of us. We will probably just take it easy this afternoon. We are supposed to be out of our hotel room by 2:00 this afternoon, then we catch a 7 p.m. bus for the hour drive to Lao Cai where we catch the 9 p.m. all-night train to Hanoi. We get off the train in Hanoi around 6 a.m., un-showered of course, hopefully meet Huang and Hung and start a three-hour drive to Halong Bay. Halong Bay has the same limestone rock formations we were seeing in Thailand at the moment the tsunami struck. Once at Halong Bay we will take a several-hour boat ride, eat lunch and take the three-hour drive back to Hanoi where we are to end up at the Hoa Binh hotel again. I doubt we will get much sleep on the train. Like I said, we have an interesting night and day ahead of us.

So far the Vietnamese have been what I expected: hardworking, enterprising and clever. They also seem more forthright than the Thai people, whom we love because they always tell us what we want to hear, even if they don't mean it or intend to do what they say they will. The Vietnamese don't seem to be like that, which is refreshing. But then again, I do like being told what I want to hear!

There is that irritating thing we have experienced, like today with the two Xe Om drivers. I agreed to pay them 50,000 dong before Linda and I got on the two cycles, and then when they dropped us off, they try to claim it was 50,000 each. I had been abundantly clear. I just scowled and walked away. It is not that uncommon in tourist situations, but irritating nonetheless.

Today when we were trekking down the trail to Cat Cat Village we were overtaking some Asian tourists, two women holding the hands of a young girl as they carefully walked down the steep steps. They were gingerly walking around some animal poop on the trail. I heard one of the women say some words in a foreign language ending with "goat sheet". "Goat sheet?" the little girl repeats inquiringly. Yes, "goat sheet".

Back to last night and our fun time with Melinda and Amanda. They used an expression I didn't understand, but could intuit. They were meaning to say "easy as pie" or something similar. "Piece of piece" was what I heard. I asked them to repeat it. "Piece of piece". They could see I was still confused, so they spelled it out for me: "piece of piss". What the hell? Where does that come from? They had no idea and acknowledged it is a pretty weird, but common, Aussie expression. Of course, where does "easy as pie" come from?

Linda and I have been sitting at our lobby fireplace location in our Sapa hotel. It is now about 5:30 p.m. I am eating a snack. We saw Melinda and Amanda a short while ago returning, exhausted, from a day of sightseeing. They will join us shortly.

THURSDAY, NOVEMBER 30

Hung, our driver, and Huang, our guide for northern Vietnam.

Linda and I are sitting having breakfast on the familiar grounds of the Hoa Binh hotel in Hanoi. It is just past 6 a.m.

The overnight "Victoria Express" train pulled into Hanoi Station at 5:30 a.m. We have come back to the hotel from the train station to drop our bags off, freshen up and have some breakfast before we leave in a short while to begin the 3½ hour drive to Halong Bay. We will board a boat for a four-hour cruise and then drive back to Hanoi. We should get back to the Hoa Binh Hotel around 7 p.m. Maybe in time for a $7 massage?

Last night, the bus left the Victoria Hotel in Sapa around 7 p.m. and we rode down the mountain to the Lao Cai train station with an English couple. We arrived to the station about an hour early, so we loaded our bags, checked in to the train and walked back out of the train station to hang out in the square in front of it.

Several vendors had set up tables with sodas and beers and snacks for sale. We sat at one and ordered two canned Hanoi beers and watched a little two-year old boy playing around in all the hustle and bustle of the square. As it turned out, there were several little one- to three-year old boys in the immediate area being watched by their two young mothers. Linda took a couple of pictures and handed me the camera so I could show the boys, their mothers and grandmothers the pictures on the screen of the digital camera. Linda thought the little boys were cute---and they were. I thought the mothers were cute, too. It was a very fun and happy interaction with all of them.

We walked back into the train station and the train left right on schedule at 9:15 p.m.

The train ride was uneventful. I took an Ambien and slept pretty comfortably all night. The sleeper compartment had two beds with a narrow space between them. The beds were 6 inches too short for me, but I made do.

The Victoria Hotel in Sapa was very nice. Probably too nice. We will be staying in four Victoria hotels this trip. In addition to the one in Sapa, we will stay in them at Hoi An and two in the Mekong Delta. They are elegant hotels built to fit into the culture and style of their surroundings; at least, that is what I gather from the one in Sapa and the literature I have read. These hotels remind us in that regard of the small chain of hotels in which we stayed in Thailand, the Anantara hotels in the Golden Triangle and Ko Samui (and we ate Christmas dinner at the one at Kao Lok which was destroyed the next day by the tsunami). Linda has been complaining about our Hanoi hotel, the Hoa Binh, where I am sitting now. This clean, efficient hotel doesn't meet her standards apparently. We have two more nights in it so she will have to make do. She is way too pampered for this kind of travel at times.

Time to head out for Halong Bay.

FRIDAY, DECEMBER 1

Halong Bay

It is now Friday afternoon and I have been walking Hanoi all morning and then some. I just stopped for some lunch; it is 2 p.m. Let me catch up on yesterday.

The drive to Halong Bay from Hanoi was broken up by a couple of stops. We made a stop at a facility where handicapped people made various crafts, mostly lacquered plates and paintings and intricately woven textile art pieces. We bought a woven textile for $125 US (an art piece I think we are going to love) and a lacquered plate for about $20 US. Some of the people doing the work, which we were able to experience firsthand as we walked through their workplaces, were visibly handicapped or disfigured. But, others appeared okay which may have meant they were deaf. For sure they had their eye sight and mental acuity because of the intricacy of their work---pretty impressive stuff.

We also stopped at a ceramic factory and watched people hand craft individual bowls, pots and plates and then hand paint them. It was hard to believe the number of individual pieces that were in the little warehouse. There were six women working at six stations. We watched them. They work fast, meticulously and with smiles on their faces.

A portion of the drive to Halong Bay from Hanoi took us through a coal mining area. Boy, talk about black dust! Most people we saw, though, not everyone, wore masks to protect them from the black dust that roiled off the street. It was pretty dirty for about ten miles.

We were told this part of Vietnam is known for its production and it was evident from the number of working facilities we saw and the amount of goods being transported along the highway. Unlike in the mountains, here there was a lot of rice field activity since the warmer climate allows more than one planting a season. We passed numerous motorcycles carrying live animals in cages precariously strapped to the small two-wheeled vehicles; cages of live chickens, pigs and in one case, dogs, being hauled to the market for sale and slaughter. I cringed when I saw the basket of five or six dogs; thank God Linda was looking down reading. Just a few minutes earlier she was all upset that they were cramming cute live pigs into cages. Huang couldn't understand why Linda would be so concerned about the comfort of the pigs that would not see the next sunset. Linda was suggesting they should at least get a "last meal"! I knew better than to say it, but was thinking, that is exactly what they are going to have!

The boat ride on Halong Bay was unremarkable. Huang, Linda and I were the sole guests on a 40-foot boat which slowly cruised us out to a couple of the 3,000 islands in Halong Bay. We de-boarded and walked through two of the scores of caves on the various islands. The caves were very ho-hum.

Afterwards, we cruised to one of the floating homes of one of the fishing families. We saw their submerged cages holding live fish, squid, shrimp and crabs. They had four or five different kinds of crab all much more colorful and cool looking than our Dungeness.

We re-boarded and were fed a many-course seafood lunch as we cruised around. The crabs served us were small and a little messy to crack and get meat from. The lady attendant/server on the boat had placed a bowl of water with sliced limes on the table. When Linda took the crab meat she had dug out of the crab's shell and reached over to dip it into the water bowl to wash off the green innards that were clinging to the meat, the lady attendant shrieked, diving toward Linda to prevent her from dousing her food in what was intended to be a finger bowl for washing our hands. Huang explained to Linda she shouldn't wash the green stuff off (never mind not using the "wash basin") because it was simply "crab fat" and was meant to be eaten. Linda made it clear she didn't care what they called it, it was crab "guts" to her and she wasn't eating that "shit". I didn't blame her. But, not wanting to be similarly chastised, I ate mine.

We got back to Hoa Binh Hotel in Hanoi about 6:30 p.m. pretty exhausted. We both showered and I went for my 1½ hour, $7 massage. When I got back to the hotel, we went out for dinner. It was nearly midnight when my head hit the pillow.

I paid more attention to driving techniques yesterday. It dawned on me that as good a driver as Hung seems to be, he never looks in his mirrors. Likewise for motorcyclists pulling into a street; the driver doesn't look back at oncoming traffic, he merely pulls into the traffic slowly, deliberately and predictably. The expectation is that it is the responsibility of oncoming drivers to avoid what is merging in front of them, not for the motorcyclist to worry about what is behind him. This would explain why Hung doesn't look in his mirror---he doesn't view it as his job! Less than half of the motorcycles even have mirrors and when they do, they are generally pulled up to look over the driver's shoulder rather than around the driver's arm because traffic travels so closely together, mirrors sticking out beyond the handle bars get knocked off.

On several occasions yesterday, we saw one, two or a herd of five or six cows walking down the highway, or simply crossing it. Mind you, these are very busy thoroughfares with speeds in the 25 to 50 mph range. Just like with everything else, the traffic just parts around the lumbering cows with no adverse reaction. Not seeing any "minders", we assume these cows simply know their routine: "Okay ladies, the sun is going down, it is time to take our beefy butts across this here human trail and go home to our rice paddy."

As crazy as this Vietnam world is to us, it works pretty damned well.

Before I left the hotel this morning, I took time to send the following email home:

HANOI, VIETNAM
Subject: Greetings from Vietnam

Xin Chao!

That means either "hello" or "let's get naked and ride a water buffalo". I will let you know next time.

Linda is complaining about the lack of 5-star accommodations (what does she want?... her hair dryer works!) and Gary is nagging at her for being a pain in the ass, so I guess we are doing great! If not, at least things are normal! We are both healthy, although a wee bit weary, and enjoying ourselves.

We are back in Hanoi for a couple of days before flying off very early Saturday morning to Hue, in the middle of Vietnam near the former DMZ (former, although I hope it is still de-militarized!). The last time I wrote we were in Sapa in the very north near China in the mountains near Vietnam's highest peak (10,000'). Beautiful country with those incredible terraced rice fields cascading down the side of steep mountains you see in pictures all the time. There we trekked miles along trails to be among several of the tribes of Vietnam...elaborately dressed in the colorful clothing and remarkably humble in their living. Nonetheless, strikingly attractive and bright big smiles. And the children...of course toddlers are cute the world over, but my God...adorable.

We took an all night train back to Hanoi two nights ago which was surprisingly comfortable despite the 5-1/2' bed; I was actually able to sleep (I am discovering Ambien is very effective!). We had, of course, the most luxurious accommodations the train had to offer...we understand the other coaches may have been less comfortable...unless you are cool with baskets full of live chickens in the seat next to you...I am not sure even Ambien would have helped with that.

We were met at 5:30 am by our driver and took off immediately for a 3-1/2 hour long drive to Halong Bay. Halong Bay is another postcard recognizable place with the limestone islands jutting up from the water. We cruised out to one of the islands and walked through a couple of the caves which sounds more daring and interesting than it was. But they served us traditional Vietnamese seafood on board and it was a pleasant day on board even though it was overcast and gray out.

Linda is being her normal entertaining self. To the abject horror of the Vietnamese attendant she dipped her crab meat into the water set out to wash our hands to wash the "guts" off the crab meat before putting it in her mouth. The "guts", which they consider the "fat" of the crab and of course eat. Linda made it clear she didn't care what they called that green shit, she wasn't eating it! The bewildered looks on their faces said it all....the term "Caucasian" to them must be similar to our references to "blonde". (Don't tell her, but my hand full a green-shit covered crab meat was half way to the water bowl when the attendant shrieked).

We finally got to our Hanoi hotel around 7 pm to an eagerly anticipated shower....it had been an eventful but long couple of days. Oh, and I had my 6th massage in as many days....hey, they cost $7 US...and that is for 1-1/2 hours! And yes, the extra 1/2 hour is necessary---the girls are so cute...er, small, I mean....it takes a long time for them to get from head to toe!

We have a day to explore Hanoi more today and then catch our flight south very early in the morning. I will report back from somewhere in central Vietnam.

Oh.....and the best news??? No snow in Vietnam...even at 6,000 feet! Hope you are all surviving Seattle's bad conditions!

Bye for now,

Gary

After getting that email off, I wanted to spend more time walking the Old Quarter of Hanoi today and did so for

about three hours. The streets are so incredibly congested, narrow and, in some cases, winding. I walked the various "hangs": the hang via (cloth), the hang bo (baskets), the hang giay (shoes), the hang ten (...kidding!). And suddenly I noticed I was "hanging" around a place I had already been. Somehow I had walked in a circle. So much for my great sense of direction. When it happened a second time, I realized I was so lost I didn't know where I was, none, nada. It is a 70 degree overcast today and I started feeling some sprinkles, so it seemed like a good time for an indoor activity, time for me to move on to phase two of my day, the Museum of Ethnology. Fortunately, the museum was a cab ride away. I wasn't so lost I couldn't find a cab, so that was my easy out.

The museum was very good. The part that stood out was the section devoted to the period of "bao cap", or Subsidy Economy from 1975-1986. This is not an ethnology subject, so it was odd to find it in this museum, but it was very well done. The communist subsidy economy had been in place since the 1945 revolution in the north, but was expanded to include food items after the reunification after the north won the war against the south in 1975. It was a very tough eleven-year period for the Vietnamese until the communists declared "doi moi' or "Renovation" in 1986. It goes a long way toward explaining the hard working resiliency of the Vietnamese. It makes one wonder how much good could be accomplished in the U.S. if a generation had to live on a rice allocation, rice that wasn't always available and oftentimes rank and wormy. This was only twenty years ago and the better times seen now by Vietnam has only been around ten years, max! Anyway, I think it is interesting and it gives me a deeper perspective of, and appreciation for, what I see walking the streets of Hanoi.

I saw the Martyrs' Monument near Hoan Kiem Lake as I tooled around. It honors those having died fighting for Vietnam's independence from France in 1954. One of the statues holds a pronged spear, something that is frequently seen as a symbol of Vietnam's quest for independence. The spear would explode when a man charged an enemy tank and pressed the tongs against the tank's side, killing the charging man and hopefully, for his sake, doing at least some damage to the damned tank!

Walking down "hang postcards", today, I stepped into a place to buy some postcards of images I haven't yet been able to capture with my own camera. I may scan them and use them in my photobook when I get home. The young man at the store greeted me with a "hello" and I said "xin chao". In response, he rattled off some Vietnamese that I took to be "Oh, you speak Vietnamese!?" to which I gave a quick and firm "no"! He did speak English though and we had a good chuckle and a brief conversation. As I walked out of his little store with my purchase I waved and said "gaam on", thanking him. That got another laugh out of him.

Ok, time for some more walking.

——— ——— ———

I just got back from a massage; I think I am 100%, I don't think I have missed a day yet! This girl, all of 100 pounds, is the second one to walk on my back and backs of my legs; she had good balance! I wonder if other of their customers get that treatment; I must look so big to them, they think I am a sidewalk.

When I took off earlier for more walking, I first walked back to Hoan Kiem Lake, which we had walked past several times since it was between our hotel and the Old Quarter. In the middle of the lake is Thap Rua ("tortoise tower"), an iconic image of Hanoi; it looks a bit like the top of a Medieval castle or fort sticking up from the depths of the lake. I had yet to get a photo of it and wanted one.

After that I headed to the area south of our hotel to explore more of the French District; a much seedier part of town. Unlike other parts of Hanoi we have been so far, I saw no Caucasians; locals were stopping and looking at me. We are no longer in Minnesota, honey! I never felt threatened, much more like I was a curiosity; that monkey-in-the-zoo thing.

It's hard to sit here street side (at my normal place next to the Hoa Binh Hotel), having a beer in the dark at 6:30 p.m. and fathom that in my lifetime, a mere 35 years ago, American B-52 bombers were dropping their hardware on this city; maybe on this very spot I am now sitting. In another sense, 35 years is a long time (God, I am old!) and it seems a million years ago. I don't, and haven't until now, think about the war, and the Vietnamese don't seem to either. But, why should they? The "American War", although almost twenty years long, is a mere blip on the screen of Vietnamese history. They have been occupied by the Chinese, twice, the French, twice, and Japan; not to mention an ugly three-year battle with Cambodia after they kicked the Americans out in 1975 (it was actually 1968, it just took the Americans a while to figure it out).

SUNDAY, DECEMBER 3

In the underground meeting hall of the Vinh Moc Tunnels

It is Sunday afternoon and we are in Hue. We arrived yesterday; I have some catching up to do.

Our last night in Hanoi, Friday night, before getting up early the next morning to fly to Hue, Linda and I went to dinner at a place called Hoa Sua, a place where youths are brought off the streets to be trained as chefs and waiters. The food and setting were both awesome. I suspect we might venture back there our last night in Vietnam before we fly back home in a few weeks.

We had to wake up at 3:30 a.m. the next morning, Saturday, to catch our 6:30 a.m. flight to Hue. The small, modern and efficient airport in Hanoi (which I barely remember from our arrival over a week ago) was easy. Our plane bounced into Hue in a torrential downpour and low visibility. Someone forgot to tell me that it is monsoon season in central Vietnam; I must have missed that little detail in the guide book. Our guide, Ba, and driver, Tang, met us at the baggage claim in Hue and we took off in the rain.

Our first stop thirty minutes away was at the Tomb of Minh Mang, the second (1820-1840) emperor of the Nguyen Dynasty. We got out of the car onto the mucky, red-clay dirt road and hustled for cover under a tent that one of the vendors had set up outside the entrance to the tomb. We weren't dressed for the wet weather, but it was only 8 a.m. so we knew we wouldn't be able to get into our hotel room first; we needed to resort to a quick change in the parking lot in the rain. We sloshed back to the car and fumbled with our luggage in the downpour to get raincoats and more appropriate shoes. We also bought two

umbrellas from the vendor whose tent cover we had used. Drenched already, we then walked the grounds of tomb for about thirty minutes.

The emperors tended to build their mausoleums during their lifetime; the tombs tend to be extravagant, multi-structure affairs covering up to twenty acres. We saw three such tombs before heading to our hotel room around noon.

I didn't realize when I paid $2 US for each umbrella that I was actually buying water filters! How do you make an umbrella that allow water through the material? Linda and I were soaked through.

We ate lunch at our hotel in Hue, took naps. Later, Linda stayed in, and dry, at the hotel and continued her nap while I toured the remains of the Imperial Palace that sits along the Perfume River in Hue. The Palace and its grounds were destroyed during the 1968 Tet offensive during the American War so there wasn't much to see. As I toured the grounds, it was still raining, but not as hard as earlier.

By the time I got back to the hotel it was---what time was it?----that's right, massage time! Linda and I both had massages at our hotel, but not before I tried out the hotel's steam-less steam room and their Jacuzzi. They had both hot and cold water tubs, I thought I had erred when I stepped in, calf deep, to one tub; it at first felt cold, then suddenly and painfully, I realized the sensation was not cold, but heat, scalding heat! Screw that, I left the tub and went in for my massage.

We ate dinner that night at another chef-school type of Vietnamese restaurant. It was in a house on the citadel grounds and they seated us on a canopied outdoor patio surrounded by lily pad ponds with frogs (and maybe other creatures) in them. Since it was still raining, it was a very cool atmosphere. The presentation of the seven-course fixed menu was as incredible as the taste and flavors. It was a great meal and a great evening.

I commented earlier that Ho Chi Minh was revered in the North and affectionately called Uncle Ho. Well, our guide, Ba, a former lieutenant in South Vietnam's army during the American War condescendingly called him "Uncle Ho Ho Ho. He had nothing good to say about good ole Uncle Ho. "We should have won the war. We are smarter, were better trained and harder working, but the Americans abandoned us when the North continued to get support from the Russians, Chinese and North Koreans. So, they won." Ba expected to be executed after the fall of Saigon in 1975 (Ba was 25 years old then), but instead he was sent to a re-education camp. After three years of "brainwashing" (his word) that had him take a "test" and determined that he was fit to be released. I made the observation to him (based on his "Ho Ho Ho" remark) that the re-education didn't seem to stick. With a grim smile and a glare in his eyes, he said tightly, "Not one damned word." Alrighty then, time for a new topic!

This morning at 7:30 a.m. I took off with Tang and Ba in the car to drive to the DMZ (the demilitarized zone which separated North Vietnam from the South Vietnam during the American War). Linda wasn't interested and preferred to walk and shop Hue. It was about a two-hour drive north to the DMZ from Hue.

Our first stop was the town of Quang Tri where a 16th century citadel was reduced to rubble in 1972. In the spring of that year the North Vietnamese swarmed this South Vietnamese stronghold taking it and control of the whole Quang Tri province, which borders the DMZ to the south. For four months South Vietnamese artillery and U.S. B-52's bombed the city and the citadel. The South lost 5,000 men re-taking the city. Ba says the North lost 75,000 men!

Ba had been to Quang Tri, not during that conflict, but after and he said the whole province of Quang Tri was nothing but rubble; "no houses, no trees." Quang Tri province is the size of the tri-county area around Seattle. Ba pointed out that all of the houses and trees we were currently seeing were less than thirty years old. We saw only one war-ravaged building that was still standing.

We drove past Quang Tri and crossed the Ben Hai River on a bridge that was bombed out in 1967 by the U.S. Before being destroyed, the North half of the bridge was painted Red for the communists; the south half, yellow. The river was the line of demarcation between the North and the South; it was the middle of the DMZ, the 17th parallel.

The DMZ was established by the 1954 Geneva Conference between Ho Chi Minh and the French. I had Ba take my picture with the river and the new bridge to my back; I was standing on the north shore.

We continued to drive north along the shoreline of the South China Sea for ½ hour to Vinh Moc where 1½ miles of North Vietnamese tunnels remain from the war. They were built over 18 months in 1966-1967 and housed a whole village of people and Vietcong. Seventeen babies were born in these tunnels during the war. We walked through them, maybe several hundred yards worth. While these tunnels have been preserved, they are in much the same condition as when they were used. There are only a few lights and no direction signs or guides---it would be very easy to get lost or hurt inside them. There are three levels to the tunnels, the deepest is 75 feet below the surface. As we scrunched through the narrow, tiny, dark funnels, we were constantly scrambling up and down on slippery surfaces. My shoulders barely fit through the passageways and often didn't. The tunnels were 5'5" to 5'10" high.

There were occasional notched-out areas in the sides of passageways; this is where individuals, or whole families, slept. My body would not even fit in most of the notched-out bedrooms. I did hunker into one meant for a family and had Tang take my photo. Unfortunately, like with the other photos taken underground the quarters were so tight it was difficult to take pictures and it is unlikely the results will give the viewer any actual perspective of how tight and cramped everything is. There was one spot where I could stand upright; that was in a larger 8 x 15 foot room that was used for community gatherings.

Ba was having a real problem inside the tunnels. He was genuinely frightened, although he tried gamely to mask his fear, it gripped him and he couldn't wait to get out. That shortened my visit and exploration some, but not enough for me to feel like I missed anything. Both Ba and Tang (who at least was capable of stopping long enough for me to take his picture) were literally on their hands and knees breathless when we emerged from underground. It is true that the climb out of the tunnel was steep and long and both of them are smokers, but I suspect fear played a bigger part. Those

tunnels carry horrific memories for them that I can't even imagine.

From the tunnels of Vinh Moc we returned south and crossed back over the Ben Hai River. On the south shore of the river we drove upriver (west) past miles of rubber trees and pepper plants in the more hilly part of our drive and acres of rice fields along the Ben Hai valley floor. We stopped so I could take pictures of a farmer and water buffalo plowing a field right next to the road. We stood and watched the farmer with the water buffalo make a couple of circuits around his small rice paddy and could hear him talk to his buffalo, "Go left", "Stop", Tang translated for me. It was mesmerizing to watch man and animal work together I also took a picture of the only mechanized piece of farm equipment I have seen this whole trip so far; it surprised both Tang and Ba to see it.

We had gone this direction to visit the Truong Son National Cemetery where tens of thousands of communist soldiers are buried (no surprise, there are no cemeteries for the thousands of South Vietnamese who died). We got to the cemetery and walked through it. There were very few people at the cemetery---we were not in the mainstream of tourism here.

As Ba, Tang and I exited the cemetery, I was approached by a Caucasian man who also had a Vietnamese guide with him, He had been watching me as our walking paths merged to exit the cemetery and finally spoke up and asked me if I was an American. Wary, I carefully acknowledged that I was. The man then asked what I "thought of all of this", as he swept his hand over the thousands of North Vietnamese gravestones. Not sure where this line of questioning was going, I cautiously said I thought it was a very sad thing. Ba, being a former, but proud and somewhat bitter South Vietnamese Army lieutenant, interjected a little emotionally that the Americans should never have backed out of the war and had they not, "we (the South) would have won".

The man then realized the tension he was creating, shook his head apologetically and said "Don't get me wrong. I am a German from the former West Germany, and am grateful to the thousands of Americans who died in WWII so that I could enjoy the freedoms I do today. I have even visited most of the many American cemeteries in Europe." "But," he continued with a sad shrug of his shoulders and a wave of his hand toward the cemetery, "I do not understand this war."

We talked for another twenty minutes; an interesting and friendly conversation. He was curious about my teenage recollections of fearing having to go to Vietnam, of shivering at the mention of names like Quang Tri, Khe Sang, Hue and Hamburger Hill---places I heard on the television news daily as a kid and now, on this day 35 years later, was actually visiting.

Interestingly, the German was also curious to know how Jane Fonda was received in America these days due to her anti-war antics in the late 1960's. I have heard Jane Fonda's name more in the last two to three days than in the last ten years. Her open and graphic demonstrations against the Vietnam War were viewed as anti-American by many. When the German gentleman broached the topic he first asked if I had heard of John Bays. When I clarified a little, I said, do you mean Joan Baez? Yes, yes, he said. Still confused I realized he was asking the question in connection with the Vietnam War. Oh, I said, you must mean Jane Fonda. Ah, yes, that is it! Ba about threw up when he heard her name and had plenty to say about her, none of it repeatable. He hates Jane Fonda. Jane had better hope to never meet Ba in person, he would take pliers to her fingernails.

A third person mentioned Jane and in each of these cases the image of her in Hanoi during the height of the war standing behind a North Vietnamese anti-aircraft gun pretending to shoot down American flyers is one people around the world seem to remember---and be appalled by. The general message being, it is okay to oppose a war, just be sure to stand behind the young men and women risking and losing their lives fighting it.

I got back to our hotel in Hue at 1:30 p.m. I left a note for Linda in our room and walked the town of Hue, which doesn't have a lot to offer. Trashier than Hanoi it is much less busy and not very interesting. When I get back to the hotel, Linda and I sat by the hotel's pool to catch up with each other on the day's events and I have been taking the opportunity to get caught up in this journal, which I now am.

——— ——— ———

After our poolside time together, Linda and I left around 4:30 p.m. to go have side-by-side pedicures---very romantic. It is hard to believe I gave up my daily massage for a pedicure! But my toes look sweet!

We sat together and had a beer at a street side bar where Linda talked to a Dutch couple we had met in Hanoi. We seemed to be on roughly the same travel plan as they are. Later, we had drinks in our hotel bar where we talked to an English couple for quite a while. Finally, dinner---and not a very good one---at a French restaurant.

Bed time. Tomorrow we are off to Hoi An.

TUESDAY, DECEMBER 5

Victoria Hoi An Hotel with temporary fencing to protect from Typhoon Durian

Yesterday was the day of the Typhoon Durian. It hit Vietnam's coastline around 11 p.m. last night killing twenty people. At least, that was the report as of this morning. It hit the three provinces south of us hardest, hitting our current location with only the fringe of its power, so our experience was limited to just really bad weather.

We are currently in Hoi An and I am sitting in the breakfast room of the Victoria Hoi An Hotel at 8 a.m. This is the second of the four Victoria Hotels we will stay in on this trip. This is a beautiful one right on the south end of the very long China Beach. We have an extremely nice beach bungalow literally fifteen meters from the waves---and needless to say, the waves were pretty violent all afternoon yesterday, and it got worse after dark. After our tsunami near-miss in Thailand, Linda was a little anxious and wanted to change rooms away from the water, but after checking the internet to determine the location and scope of Typhoon Durian, I convinced her (and myself) it wasn't necessary.

Although the storm has now passed, it is still windy and overcast outside, but not raining. When we got to Hoi An and to our hotel yesterday about 1:30 p.m., we just stayed indoors; the weather just was not accommodating.

I took advantage of the time indoors after we arrived yesterday and used the hotel's computer to write an email home:

> ***Hoi An, Vietnam***
> *Subject: In case you were wondering.....*
>
> *....the typhoon, Durian, should miss us. It is predicted to hit the shore of Vietnam tonight about 350 km south of Hoi An where we are currently and wind speeds are estimated at around 160 km/hr. I know you are all thinking we are like bad ju-ju or something....and you might be right. But this time we were a little more clever and fooled Mother Nature by putting out the word we were going to be in Nha Trang tonight...so she steered the storm south to Nha Trang to get us...but she will miss. Just stay mum about where we REALLY are, ok? The bad news is, we are scheduled to be in Nha Trang in four days. Hope she leaves us something! We will keep you posted, but nothing for you to be concerned about...and no, Britt, you can't have the wine in my cellar....yet.*
>
> *Ok, enough of all of that.*

I did confirm that Xin Chao means hello. Riding a water buffalo naked is "gitna cjaaft az".

We spent the last couple of days in Hue, just south of the DMZ. We landed in a rain storm and have been having pretty wet weather...someone forgot to tell us that this is Central Vietnam's monsoon season. How can the North and South be having a dry season and it is monsoon season here?? We bought $2 umbrellas that work more like water filters, so having dry clothes to wear has been a challenge.

We drove south today from Hue for about three hours, first to Danang and then on to Hoi An where we just checked into our hotel after some sightseeing. It is about 2 pm on Monday, the 4th, our time, 11 pm the 3rd, Seattle time. We have an incredible bungalow fairly close to the beach where the surf is roiling pretty wildly from the typhoon. Linda is wanting to change our room...the surf is making her nervous. Aargh....real men don't change rooms, right?

The trip to the DMZ yesterday was very interesting to me, seeing sights that fortunately I didn't have to see during the war. I squeezed through former Vietcong underground tunnels barely wide enough to accommodate my shoulders and only 5'10" high at the highest points. There are three levels going as deep as 75 feet. The quarters were so cramped it was not possible to take pictures that will give the viewer any concept of the tunnel's cramped spaces. That day, we drove through miles and miles of land near and within the DMZ where there was not a building or tree older than 25 years. Everything was leveled to the ground by B-52 carpet bombing. There are still places where things won't grow and the bomb craters are evident everywhere.

Our guide while in central Vietnam is a former Lieutenant in the South Vietnamese Army. When the North overran Saigon in 1975, his life was spared and he was sent to a re-education camp for three years. He has told us several very interesting stories. Since there is risk of reprisals and a reasonable chance that you all may not be the only ones to read this email, even to this day, I will save more stories about that until we get home.

In the past when I would see the ubiquitous post cards of the Vietnamese farmer in his conical hat in flooded rice paddies to his knees guiding a hand-made ancient single blade plow behind a water buffalo, the skeptic in me assumed if the photographer had panned his camera 90 degrees in either direction, you would see a, perhaps battered, Ford tractor pulling a tired old four blade John Deere plow. Not so, I now know. We have driven hundreds of miles thus far throughout North and Central Vietnam, and with only one exception,

I have yet to see anything mechanized in any field and nothing other than man-made tools. Eighty percent of the 84 Million people in Vietnam work in agriculture and this little country is the second largest exporter of rice in the world....all fertilized by water buffalo shit. Is that why we tend to eat potatoes (is that with, or without, the 'e'?)?

Sorry to be so long winded....but it is stormy outside and nothing better to do at the moment! We are having a great time. I am really enjoying the food and even getting fairly adept at using chopsticks. It became a lot easier once I figured out that the two sticks were to go in one hand, not one in each hand! The people are pleasant, helpful and fun, and everything thus far has moved along as planned.

I will report back soon so no one will worry....and to keep Britt out of my wine cellar.

Gary

When we arrived in Hoi An yesterday and decided to stay indoors, I also was recovering a little from motion sickness; the three-hour drive from Hue to Hoi An was difficult for me in the back seat of the car.

About 1½ hours out of Hue south on the way to Danang, we drove over the Hai Van pass, a winding, narrow road that spirals its way through the Truong Son Mountains that jut into the South China Sea (Ba tells us that the Vietnamese refuse to call the sea anything other than the Pacific Ocean; "China doesn't own the sea!"). Normally a beautiful drive, the weather was so bad you couldn't see forty meters. The last mile before reaching the top of the pass and dropping down the other side, it got to the point we couldn't see even two meters in front of the car. On that very narrow, twisting road with a huge drop off on one side, it was a fairly hairy drive. Tang, bless his heart, drove very slow, I mean like five mph and followed the white line, which the road fortunately had, probably because the pass is known as "Cloudy Pass" indicating bad visibility is not unusual.

We learned as we inched our way over Cloudy Pass that they recently completed the tunnel through the mountain that provided for a straight, smooth, easy 6 kilometer drive over the mountains rather than the 20 kilometer nauseating adventure we were on. As Ba divulged the tunnel option we failed to take, he said, "but there is no view in a tunnel!" He said this as we all were peering through the opaque windows of the car trying to see the road! After another hour of treacherous driving we got to Danang; by then I was really not feeling well.

Oops, so much for no rain today---and the power just went off---and on---and off again. It is now a torrential downpour outside. Reminds me of how hard it rained on us in the Amazon; at least here I am indoors. Power is on again.

I have to take a break now and decide what we are going to do today.

——— ——— ———

Rained out! We left breakfast this morning and talked with Ba about the plans for the day. We were to see the town of Hoi An in the morning and then drive 75 kilometers to My Son, an old Champa political center from the 4th century to the 13th century; the Champa equivalent to Angkor Wat in Cambodia. However, in 1969, that area was a North

Vietnamese stronghold and an important supply station for the Ho Chi Minh Trail, so despite the pleadings from scientists around the world, President Nixon ordered it bombed, destroying it. There's nothing to see now and the drive to get to it is long and winding---not my favorite thing. Especially, if the weather is going to be so bad you can't really see the countryside.

When we left the hotel this morning, the rain had eased and the wind had died down, so we had an enjoyable first hour of seeing Hoi An's old quarter; the second hour it started pouring and continues to now at noon. So, no road trip to My Son; we are back at the Victoria Hotel.

Hoi An oozes charm and culture on every street. It was Southeast Asia's major trading port from the 17th to the 19th century and there is a huge Chinese influence here; it is a great place to have suits and clothes made very well and inexpensively. Hopefully, we will have some "dry" time to enjoy the old quarter before we leave here.

My God, it is raining hard again right now! Blowing hard, too.

I forgot to mention that after our encounter with the German in the cemetery, Ba turned to me and said that I would have been a good officer in the U.S. Army. There had been no conversation leading up to his comment so I was surprised---and puzzled. He said I was smart and cool under fire. I didn't pursue the conversation with him, but I assumed at the time he was referring to the encounter with the German. That was confirmed yesterday driving to Hoi An with Linda in the car; he told Linda that I was officer material; I had really handled that German! I think that experience and conversation had a big impact on Ba.

During yesterday's car journey, Ba also told Linda and me a story from his war days. As a lieutenant he was told by his superior officer to secure the Khe Sang hill shortly after it was occupied by the Americans. This hill at Khe Sang was later to become famous for having the war's bloodiest battle---500 Americans and 10,000 North Vietnamese died. As instructed, Ba took the 75 soldiers under his command and scouted the base of the hill---and then got lost. He had forgotten his compass. It was very dry and there was no water. Finally, almost to a critical stage without water for him and his men, they spotted a water hole, a spring presumably. Fearing an ambush, Ba staged his men with guns ready strategically around the water hole and then allowed his men two or three at a time to drink from the pond. Ba was the last to go get his drink. After quenching his massive thirst, he noticed something in the bottom of the pond. He ordered one of his men to dive down to investigate. What Ba had seen were skulls, human skulls. The pond was full of corpses.

Ba kept it quiet from his men, but he was very concerned about the health hazards to him and his men from drinking the contaminated water. Once Ba and his men finally got back to the base on top of Khe Sang hill, he related his story to his superior, an American army officer. The officer handed Ba a beer and said, "Drink this and forget about it!"

I sense that Ba has a lot of war stories, some that would be hard for him to tell. He was also seriously injured when he took shrapnel from an anti-aircraft gun in his right hip. He spent three months on an American hospital ship.

We said goodbye to Ba today. We will see Tang the day after tomorrow when he drives us to the Danang airport for our flight to Nha Trang. Ba has a wedding to attend, so we won't see him again. He was quite the character!

_____ _____ _____

We are really hunkered down. It's about 5 p.m. and it is still raining sideways, much of the time, like right this minute---in torrents.

Since it has been too stormy to do anything else, I decided to walk China Beach. This is the same China Beach we know as the place U.S. servicemen took their R&R during the American War, except we are at its opposite, southern, end. The servicemen played in the sand twenty kilometers north of here in Danang. The beach is flat and has nice fine sand. It would be perfect for jogging, but I walked---about 3½ miles. On the way out, heading north, my back and right side got rain-soaked by the sideways wind off the sea, on the way back, things got evened out; my front and left side took the brunt of the weather. It was a good exercise walk, but nothing to see but sand and waves. I got back and went to the hotel's gym for an hour; the most exercise I have had in days. I won't be able to move tomorrow. I then sat in the hotel's steam room for a while. Yes, my (new titanium) hip is doing well! Thanks for asking.

Ba was telling us about government corruption and censorship. About how people are not allowed to talk about politics or religion and how there are spies everywhere ready to report people who do. Ba has been prone to bad information and exaggeration (for example, 9,000,000 North Vietnamese didn't die in the war, 1,000,000 did; Hai Van pass is not 2,000 meters high, it is 500), but for what it is worth, he talks about how everyone fears each other. He has lived in the same house in Danang all his life and doesn't know his neighbors because people are afraid to talk to each other. So, last night, I am reading the Vietnamese newspaper (in English) and it speaks of one of the government ministers getting input from the people. The article acknowledged that corruption was present but said an equal issue was waste by the people and how "negative phenomena" was an issue at the "grass roots level". In another article praising the decision to increase salaries to the people, it acknowledged the need to do more for the very poorest as it would help stem "negative phenomena". Man, this all makes one appreciate the U.S. government despite its failings! And our press despite its.

WEDNESDAY, DECEMBER 6

Woman collecting wood and coconuts on China Beach at Hoi An

It is another gloomy, windy day although no rain yet this morning. Yesterday after I said that, it started raining sideways ten minutes later and never let up. I'll be going into Hoi An's old quarter today regardless of the weather.

More on the Vietnamese government: again, yesterday's newspaper had an article in which "negative phenomena" was mentioned. It is very interesting to me. After dinner last night we sat in the bar with the hotel's general manager, Claude Balland. He is a Frenchman working for a French company. He bought us a drink and we talked about his life in Vietnam. First, he said the Victoria Hotels in Southeast Asia are built on land leases and will revert back to the Vietnamese government in fifty years. According to Claude, the hotels are making very good money for his company. He confirmed Ba's story about spies; he says they are actually plain clothes policemen. He said he knows the government watches everything he does; visitors to his home get questioned about him and vice versa, he gets questioned about visitors he has to his home. It is quite oppressive. I wonder how he deals with it, but after twelve years here, he seems to like it. He has no intention of leaving.

I sent the following email home letting people know we are okay:

> ***HOI AN, VIETNAM***
> *Subject: Typhoon Durian*
>
> *Durian has safely passed us by and has been downgraded. It hit our province and the three south of us and apparently caused 20 deaths. No real drama for us although the waves were crashing just 10 to 15 meters away from our bungalow...from which we didn't move. Weather is still bad today, overcast and windy, and will likely be for another day or so. Now I can use my water filter umbrella....inverted!*
>
> *We will check back in with you all again soon.*
>
> *Gary*

We also talked last night to an Australian couple as they were checking into the hotel. He is a recently retired gynecologist/obstetrician and she an emergency registered nurse. They invited us to eat dinner with them, which we did. They were a very nice couple.

Our hotel's manager, Claude, having worked throughout Southeast Asia at one time or another in his career told us how much he enjoyed working with the Vietnamese in comparison with the other Southeast Asian cultures. He credited a former French general in assessing the three major cultures in the former French Indochina: "The Vietnamese will plant the rice; the Cambodians will watch it grow; the Laotians will listen to it grow and the Thai eat the rice."

THURSDAY, DECEMBER 7

Linda is offered a ride through the flooded streets of Hoi An

It is a Maui-like morning in Hoi An. I am up early to go into the Old Quarter for the second and hopefully final fitting of the two-piece business suit and dress shirt I purchased and had tailored. The total cost for everything: $280 US. Not a big number, but I wonder how often I will wear a suit in the future. I am sure I will get some use out of it.

Let me catch up on yesterday. We spent the morning until about 2 p.m. in Hoi An, walking the portion of town that was not flooded. It is not uncommon for the Thu Bon River that flows through Hoi An to rise and flood the first street or two nearest it. The river has steadily been rising from the typhoon-inspired rains and had flooded the street nearest the river. No problem; the long, slender river canoes paddled mostly by elderly women were available to transport people to un-flooded stores and restaurants on flooded streets. Unfortunately, there was a lot of garbage floating around, too.

We had a great lunch at a place called "Mango" that had,

by virtue of the flooding, become a waterfront café. Normally, a street and a small pier fronted it, but today we floated right up to it. We sat and had a great lunch while watching the waitress sweep away the cockroaches that were also coming in for a little lunch, and a dry spot. Despite the flooded town, it was a dry day; no rain. It was very nice to have no rain and wind!

We came back to the hotel after lunch yesterday and I sat on our bungalow's deck fifteen meters from a much calmer surf and read until my 4 p.m. massage. Linda had a neck and shoulder massage, too, and afterward we went into the Old Quarter for my first fitting and dinner. The water levels in Hoi An continued to rise and we were unable to get to Club Cargo, our intended dining location for the night. It was right next to Mango, where we had lunch, and had probably 6 inches of water covering its floor. We weren't aware of that at lunchtime because we didn't get inside then to see it.

Unable to eat at Club Cargo, we opted for "Before & Now", a back street café which was now at water's edge. We sat on that café's street side porch and watched as families rode down the street, four people on a motorcycle at times, to the flood water's edge to see their town's flood waters like they had never seen it before. We know these floods aren't that uncommon, but maybe there isn't anything else for them to do! We also watched locals scurry back and forth hauling merchandise from flooded stores, presumably to store things temporarily at a higher location. Even in the relatively short time we sat having dinner, we watched the water rise another 5" – 7".

Off to the Old Quarter to get my suit.

____ ____ ____

I am back at the hotel in Hoi An again now with Linda.

I taxied to Old Quarter, picked up my tailored suit and shirt and took a Xe Om back. It had been absolutely beautiful weather this morning until I sat my butt down on the back of the motorcycle with my new suit in hand. The minute I did, it started to rain. Not hard, but doing 20 mph on a motorcycle gets you wet fast. Of course, it stopped raining the moment I got off the motorcycle back at the hotel.

Our ride comes at 12:30 p.m. today to take us to Danang's airport for our 2:15 p.m. flight to Nha Trang. Time for me to get ready to leave.

FRIDAY, DECEMBER 8

Beautiful evening beach setting at the Ana Mandara Hotel in Nha Trang

We have bitten into a little bit of heaven here. I am sitting at breakfast on the beach watching the waves roll in on a spectacular morning at the Ana Mandara Hotel in Nha Trang.

We had an uneventful transfer from Hoi An to here. A new guide (Hung) and Tang picked us up on schedule at our Hoi An hotel and drove us the ½ hour to the Danang Airport. The plane departed and landed on schedule and we were greeted after collecting our luggage by Vy, another guide arranged by BA Tours. We were checked into our rather luxurious and elegant hotel and walking its grounds and the beach by 5:30 p.m.

After checking our new hotel and its surroundings out, we sat alongside the beach at the hotel's pool/beach bar and had a beer. It was very peaceful and comfortable. After so many days of bad weather, we really enjoyed the warm, calm evening. The tiki torches were lit, a Vietnamese duo were playing stringed instruments (that wonderful

Southeast Asian music); all of that mixed with the gentle sound of the sea. It was otherwise quiet with few people around. We wondered why it was so quiet. Linda thought it might be because everyone else was inside getting cleaned up after a day on the beach. Could be. I went for a swim myself.

After a long while of enjoying the setting at the beach bar, we decided to go into the town of Nha Trang to eat at a traditional Vietnamese restaurant that had been recommended to us. I went in and showered after my salt water swim and we were soon off on the ten-minute ride to the restaurant.

The restaurant was rustic. Linda had an uncertain look on her face and I was delighted to see almost all Vietnamese customers at the tables. The popular thing seemed to order the barbeque, which means they bring your own little barbeque to your table and you cook your own meat. This had to be something adopted from when the Americans were here during the war. Linda won the heart of the guy waiting on us and he stood there and cooked our meal for us, service no one else was getting, for sure! He was great; Linda and I both really enjoyed our meal and time there.

After we finished eating, I struck up a conversation with a young couple we recognized from the Ana Mandara Hotel, the only other Caucasian couple at the restaurant. Steph and Dan had just graduated from Australia's version of law school and were traveling for a month together before starting their year-long “internship” in March. Both were 23 years old and had been dating for 3½ years; they were very mature and easy to talk to. We talked for quite a while at the restaurant and then shared a cab to a little beach front bar to have a beer before heading back to our hotel around midnight.

SUNDAY, DECEMBER 10

The results of Linda's cooking class at the Ana Mandara Hotel in Nha Trang

It is 8:30 a.m. and I am sitting at breakfast at the Ana Mandara Hotel in Nha Trang.

The last two days, Friday and Saturday, were beautiful weather days. Yesterday was almost perfect; no wind and the sea was remarkably calm. A very nice change from the bad weather we had been having. Each of the last two days, I got up around 6:30 a.m. and went for long walks on the beach, followed by a swim in the sea. Then I would sit on the beach, drink the hot

tea I would make in our room and read. Linda would join me and we would hang on the beach, swimming, reading, napping and getting sun-burned.

Both days around 2:30 p.m., I took one of the hotel's mountain bikes to explore the town of Nha Trang. The hotel's bikes were fancy with double suspension; it drew attention because you just don't see bikes like that around here. Each day, before returning to the hotel from my bike ride at around 5:30 p.m., I stopped at different hole-in-the-wall places to get massages. $8 US, including tip, and they were good ones!

I would get back to the hotel and shower and Linda and I would mosey down to the pool bar where we would sit, mostly alone, and talk with the Vietnamese hotel staff. Last night I took some time, since Linda's pedicure took a little longer than expected, and shot off a group email home.

NHA TRANG, VIETNAM
Subject: Good Morning, Vietnam!

Hello everyone....thought I would give you all a break and stay away from the computer for a few days.

After the Typhoon Durian passed by us we had real bad weather in Hoi An for a couple of days...so we were pretty hunkered down....sideways rain doesn't add much to the fun of sightseeing. More than that, though, the roads and town were flooded, so we pretty much stayed nearby the hotel.

From Hoi An we flew south 300 or 400 miles to Nha Trang for six days of relaxing in the sun...and boy is it beautiful here. The weather is gorgeous and the resort has all the best Asia has to offer. I am feeling a little antsy because I intended to come here exhausted from other travel, but the two slow days in Hoi An make me feel like I am not doing enough. Linda reminds me we have a pretty active two weeks once we leave here...and you know, she is right....so, "excuse me miss, yes, I will have another beer thank you...and please send the young lady over for my foot massage".

I fear we may be between typhoons. I read where Typhoon Linda is headed toward the Mekong Delta. I was puzzled because I knew that...hell, I am taking her there....I wondered how they knew it. Then I realized they were talking about another, less destructive, one. Haven't tracked her lately in the papers, so I am not sure...perhaps she fizzled out (the other Linda...mine…is still going strong). I don't think the Mekong Delta would be much fun....or even possible.... with high winds, so we will keep our eye on Typhoon Linda....there may have to be a change in plans, which would disappoint me.

Despite having some slow time the past few days we are loving Vietnam, and have been doing what we do, and enjoy, most....mingling with the natives. The bad news? I have not had any opportunity to practice Vietnamese. Literally everyone speaks some English....at least enough....and they insist on using it. I find myself getting lazy and not forcing their language on them. Maybe it's the blank looks I get when I try to speak Vietnamese...I apparently don't even get close!! Hey, if I can say "hello" and "thank you" in Hungarian, I should be able to do it in Vietnamese....backwards!

Travel always gives us a greater appreciation for things we have and things American. This trip has put some emphasis on government for me. It is true that one does tend to wonder about an American system that can put a peanut farmer, a Hollywood actor, an intern-baiting cigar lover and GW in its top position, but man o' man.....this communist government stuff is a whole 'nother world. And I love the fact that people (yes, you Dennis) can feel strong disgust for our president and be able to speak their mind. It's healthy, it's fun, it's good...and we take it for granted....it sure as hell wouldn't be happening here!! This is not news to anyone who has had experience behind the iron curtain, but I haven't, so it has been a wee bit of an eye opener. More on all that later....I don't want to encourage a visit from the local authorities while I am here.

Ok, everyone.....I will report in again in a few days. Hope all is well.

Gary

Both of the last two nights we ate at the hotel. Two nights ago they had a Vietnamese food buffet for $25 US per person; expensive, but very good. I almost failed to get my fill though because I was trying my best to stretch out the dining experience as long as possible so I would have more room to try more things. We got into a conversation with a couple from Munich and I was suddenly hearing the equivalent of "last call" for the food! The Vietnamese staff was very cute; they scurried around to get me things I hadn't tried and brought me plates of food---and dessert.

So we sat and ate and had a great conversation with Reiner and Petra and then moved with them to the hotel bar where we sat from 11 p.m. until well past midnight. He is an architect who designs interiors for executive jets and is old enough to remember being bombed at the end of WWII (he must be 70 or so). She was younger, very attractive and delightful. Among other very interesting things we discussed was her concern that the German language was getting "Anglicized". It was a great, fun evening.

Then, last night, Dan and Steph joined us first for drinks at the hotel bar (next to two Vietnamese women who were strumming their stringed instruments playing that great Asian music) and eventually dinner at the hotel's restaurant.

They are a seriously fun couple, both attractive, mature and intelligent. They leave today to take the bus to Dalat. We will miss them; we spent a lot of time with them while here. I got their email addresses so they can tell me about their trip to Dalat and their next stop, Angkor Wat in Cambodia.

As we sat on the patio of the restaur ant last night having dinner with Dan and Steph, the rain squalls started. And, boy, did it pour. It added a fun atmosphere to the evening, but unfortunately, the bad weather is continuing today. I got up a little later this morning, around 7:30, intending to go for a couple-hour bike ride; a combination of exploring the northern part of Nha Trang and exercise. The sideways rain discouraged me. Sitting now at breakfast, I am trying to make a plan for the day. It rains, then the sun shines, the sea is rough and now the wind is gusting; not sure what to expect weather-wise. But we need some activity, so I will figure something out.

Nha Trang is known as the place that makes the "fish sauce" used in many Vietnamese dishes. Each night off the shore we can see scores of fishing boats, old wooden 35' to 40' boats, with powerful lights shining into the water to attract shrimp into their nets. An interesting nighttime sight.

——— ——— ———

It turned out to be a pretty active day. I pushed weights around for an hour in the hotel's gym after my morning coffee and then after several false starts I took off on a hotel bike for a little touring. Every time I got up to go on the bike a rain squall would start. So, I would decide to go later; then just as quickly, the sun would come out. I'd get the bike out and ready and then....rain squall! Finally, I just said "screw it" and went. Fortunately, the rain didn't last long and it was dry for about two hours. I rode north along the beach road for 4 to 5 miles and then turned back and cycled through various city streets inland from the beach. I saw the Big Pagoda, the Big Buddha and both markets Nha Trang is known for.

Tourists who come to Nha Trang apparently don't leave the beach; I never saw another tourist the entire two hours I was gone. I never felt like I was in places during my ride I shouldn't be or wasn't safe, but It would not have been appropriate to stop and take pictures---so I didn't. I did stop and watch 8 or 9 adolescent boys play a game they appeared to be inventing as they went along that involved the triple jump. They were on a vacant, garbage-strewn lot near the bay where the fishing fleet is moored (most of the fishing goes on at night). I went through alleys and crowded streets and saw a little bit of everyday life. Pretty humble, dirty by our standards; a lot of tough living here, I suspect.

I got back to the hotel about 12:30 p.m. because I wanted to catch the last of Linda's Vietnamese cooking class. She was have a grand time, as were the hotel staff she was cooking with. It was a very informal setting; she was the only "student". I looked on as the cooks were showing Linda how to make spring rolls and both the Mango Salad and the Papaya Salad. Although they were all Vietnamese they spoke enough English to tell her what to do and to answer her questions. It was a fun and light atmosphere

and everyone (I am guessing more than normal or needed) from the kitchen and the wait staff were getting involved. Linda was cute as hell and having the time of her life. And then we sat down and ate the goods. Wow, was it ever good, seriously.

Even before the cooking class she was known by the entire hotel staff who referred to her as "Miss Linda". They all know me, too, but only because I am with her; I am Mr. Gary (better than Mr. Linda, I suppose).

Linda got roped into agreeing to a "special" two-hour massage for the price for one hour at our hotel and then decided I should do it instead of her. It was a much fancier situation than to what I have become accustomed; I usually pay $10 US or less, this was $65 US. The massage was, in fact, noticeably better and extremely relaxing. I was given a robe to wear to and from the locker room; a robe meant for a midget. The front part barely closed around my body and it didn't even go down to mid-thigh. I felt like a stripper. But, I am thinking, no big deal, I can just hold it together for the short distance I had to go. It wasn't that simple.

After the massage, she hands me back my midget robe; I put it on and grasp the front to hold it together to hide the "goods". She walks me to a sitting area to have post-massage tea, a formality to which I am totally unfamiliar. It was an Asian sitting area with pillows on the floor and occupied by two other women, who appear to be Japanese and who had on robes that actually fit. They can't keep themselves from giggling when they see me; I must look like a damned cartoon character. They are sitting all lady-like with their tea tray on the pillow in front of them. I am directed to pillows facing them within feet where I am supposed to sit. They try, totally unsuccessfully, to keep straight faces as they watched me struggle to come up with a sitting maneuver that would keep my little thingy from coming out of my little robey. I actually thought I might have been successful until I heard their collective gasp, followed by silence, then uncontrollable tittering. That told me all I needed to know about how poorly I had managed to maintain any modesty. I gave them a red-faced smile and they shyly smiled back, and then started tittering again as I daintily drank the tea I didn't really want in the first place. I figured since they were there first they would be gone by the time I had to perform the equally risky stand-up maneuver. Nope, are you kidding? Those two Japanese voyeurs weren't going to miss that show. Sure enough, they didn't and I am sure they are still laughing.

TUESDAY, DECEMBER 12

Our hotel room at the Ana Mandara in Nha Trang

It is about 7:30 a.m. and I am sitting on the beach in front of the Ana Mandara Hotel after an hour-long power walk along the water's edge on the beach. I am actually a little tired, which I fear says more about my conditioning than the rigor of my exercise. It is too hard to write here on my lap, I will take this up again later.

——— ——— ———

After about an hour sitting on the beach chair reading, I have come to the hotel's beachside café for coffee and breakfast. Today is our last in Nha Trang, and it looks to be a gorgeous one. That is good, we will both get ready to leave and then head out to do some more active sightseeing.

Linda and I talked last night and concluded that our restlessness here in Nha Trang, which was intended to be the do-nothing part of our trip, results in part from the bad weather that we had in Hoi An that kept us from doing as much aggressive sightseeing as we would do normally, and the fact that we normally plan the "relax" portion of our month-long trips at the end when we are really ready for some "down time". In short, I guess we don't feel like we have "earned" any relaxation time yet on this trip. We have two more weeks of pretty busy travel, so we will get ours, but just not in the order in which we are accustomed. After this trip, after having experienced it and knowing what to expect, we probably won't have as much of a problem having "down days" in the middle of our journey. In any event, I will push for fewer of them, wherever they may fall!

Yesterday afternoon I got antsy after finishing the book I was reading. Linda was snoozing in her poolside lounge chair, so I just hopped on my trusty bike and went riding. On two different occasions, I have had Vietnamese women on motorcycles riding alongside me talking to me as I peddle down the street. On the first occasion, a couple of days ago, three girls in their twenties on two motorcycles rode along both sides of me talking to me, as best they could with their limited English. "Where you from?" "How long you stay?" Understandably, I immediately suspected they were either begging or peddling. But, not in this case, they were just being friendly and curious. Once they ran out of English words, they pulled ahead giggling and waving. Yesterday it happened again with two women, maybe in their thirties, on a motorbike.

When I took a break from riding yesterday to get something to drink and to watch the street scene from a street-side café, the young girls working there stood next to me the entire time I sat there asking me questions whenever they could think of one to ask, and when they couldn't, they stood there anyway. Tourists aren't that novel here, perhaps it's an opportunity to practice their English, or perhaps they are just curious, a trait I like in the Vietnamese.

I have been getting the "Bill Clinton" thing a lot in Vietnam. It might be, in part, because he was just in the country for an HIV/AIDS conference and was in the local news quite a bit. He seems to be generally very well liked in Vietnam. I also have heard, twice now, that I look like CNN's Anderson Cooper. The first time I had ever heard that one was from two-year old Melina Sperry just six months ago. It surprised me to hear it again over here.

Time to go do something, or nothing, not sure which!

WEDNESDAY, DECEMBER 13

The last evening at the Ana Mandara Hotel

I am now sitting at the Nha Trang airport waiting for our 7:45 a.m. flight to Ho Chi Minh City.

Yesterday, we had a relaxing last day in Nha Trang at the beach. The weather was perfect. I read a whole book and never left the hotel after my morning walk until dinner time. I didn't even have a massage!

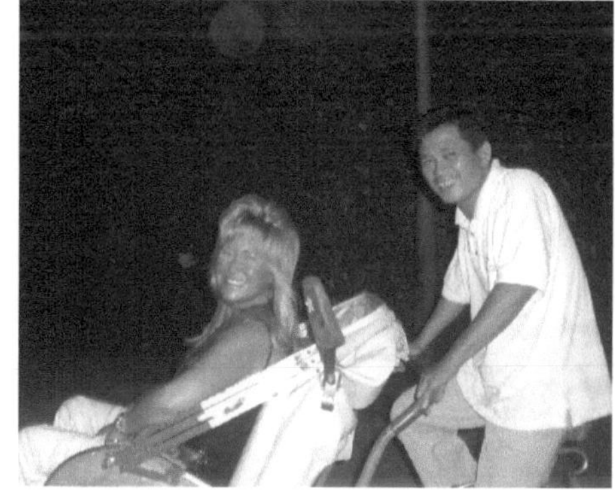

Linda and I each took a cyclo (pedi-cab where you sit in the front and get pedaled by the driver) to a restaurant in downtown Nha Trang and had a great evening meal; and once again, a great

time with the restaurant's staff. We had a very tall, adorable, twenty-one year old Vietnamese girl who spoke pretty good English wait on us. Maybe one of the pictures she insisted we take with her will end up in my photobook when I get home.

When we got back to Ana Mandara Hotel, at 9:30 p.m., it was dead as usual, so we finished packing and made sure everything was ready for our 4:30 a.m. wake-up call this morning. In the process, Linda was talking to Nguyen who was our "hostess" from the hotel during our stay. She told Miss Linda that she and Mr. Gary were everyone's favorite at the hotel because we treated everyone so nicely...and because we were so attractive! Ah, wasn't that sweet? I am somewhat surprised they find any Caucasians attractive. We did find the Ana Mandara very accommodating and a great place to stay.

THURSDAY, DECEMBER 14

A rendering of the Grand Hotel in Ho Chi Minh City

Ho Chi Minh City ("HCMC"), or Saigon, whichever is preferred, is hot and humid today. I am sitting in our hotel in HCMC, the Grand Hotel, having my morning coffee.

We landed without issue at HCMC yesterday morning about 8:30 a.m. after less than an hour flight from Nha Trang. Our new guide, Hieu, and driver, Viet, were about ten minutes late greeting us at the baggage claim. But they did show up and whisked us off to start seeing HCMC.

From the airport, we stopped first to see the former Presidential Palace, now called Reunification Palace since the Communist takeover in April 1975. We drove through the very (open) gate the North Vietnamese drove its tank over (then closed) on April 30, 1975---an iconic and symbolic image of the take-over seen and remembered around the world. The tank itself now sits on the palace grounds. Also resting on the grounds near the tank is an

American made F-4 jet which was once flown by a South Vietnamese pilot who peeled off from his squadron in 1973 (I think) and bombed the Palace instead of the Communist positions his squadron was headed for. He then defected to the North with his jet. On the roof of the Palace there are two large red circles indicating where the bombs hit; the Palace since restored, of course.

Okay, I have to interrupt my discourse. I am sitting at a breakfast table at the Grand Hotel. An Indian man joined me at my table and is currently really enjoying his breakfast---to the point of disgust! I couldn't make that much smacking noise with my mouth if I tried. Those eggs look real good rolling around inside his mouth---yum!

Anyway.....I will try to concentrate here.

We toured through the Palace and saw the conference room where the then President of South Vietnam turned the "keys to his government" over to the North's army captain on April 30. We also toured the Palace's basement with the (obviously) necessary bomb bunker and the computers, phones and maps used by the South in running their end of the way. Everything has been preserved. I forgot how archaic1975 computers and phones look! I even sat at the desk of the President of South Vietnam and pretended to use his phone.

We drove past the former U.S. Embassy where the helicopters landed on the roof on that fateful day in April 1975 extricating Americans and South Vietnamese. Like most people, I believed the photograph of people lined up on a rooftop staircase to get to the helipad to hop onto the next helicopter (the image from the play "Miss Saigon") was from the Embassy. In fact, it wasn't, it was another building, but it doesn't change the significance of the event or of the role the Embassy played in the evacuation.

Time to get moving. We are headed out of HCMC this morning.

——— ——— ———

It is now evening and am sitting at the Victoria Hotel pool bar along the Mekong River very near the Cambodian border in a town called Chau Doc. We had a long and interesting day of travel getting here, but first I need to catch up on the rest of our time in HCMC yesterday.

After visiting the Palace and passing by the U.S. Embassy in HCMC yesterday, with our guide, Hieu, in the lead, we went to the Ben Thanh market, a large, indoor market built in 1914. Linda purchased some $8 US sandals and we decided to leave there to get some lunch. We picked up a sandwich at a bakery and took it to the 5-star lobby of the 5-star Caravel Hotel. We went there in search of a fingernail place capable of taking care of Linda's 5-star acrylic fingernails. Nope, they couldn't do it

there. So, of course, it is now all about finding a place to do whatever Linda needs done to her damned fingernails. In short order, Hieu helped us find a place down the street. As usual, this process required a lot of interaction with locals and seeing shops and how locals live and was interesting despite my frustration spending so much time with it.

Hieu and I left Linda at her nail place and went to the Grand Hotel to get Linda and me checked in and to drop our luggage off. Then Hieu and I went off to HCMC's Cholon district, essentially Chinatown. We viewed an important pagoda and then walked through Binh Tay Market, Chinatown's market, a wholesale market. I have seen a lot of markets and this proved to be one of the more amazing. This was a merchandise market, so I didn't experience the gut-wrenching sights and smells of some Asian markets I have experienced, but boy, did I see merchandise! If this place didn't have it, it likely didn't exist. The photographs won't likely do justice to the extent

to which things were crammed into small places and piled into larger spaces. How do the merchants keep track of the things they have? Or find, or uncover it? In most stalls the merchants were virtually covered in their merchandise. It is truly nuts. Somehow they make it work.

Hieu dropped me off at the Grand Hotel about 2 p.m. and I went for a walk. I wanted to check out places like the Majestic Hotel and the Rex Hotel, both of which were made famous during the American War. It was hot and humid and after a while I realized I didn't feel very good;

something like heat stroke or something. I returned to the hotel, laid down for an hour in the coolness of our hotel room. That made me feel enough better to go get a massage. But even then, I basically didn't feel that well again until this morning.

Nonetheless, Linda and I joined up about 5:30 p.m. at our hotel's rooftop bar where I watched three tugs turn a huge freighter around in the Saigon River across the street from our hotel. This must be something they do all the time because they deftly engineered an impressive 180 degree spin turn in the middle of a river that is just barely wider than the ship was long. Then Linda and I got into a fun conversation with a recently retired Special Forces guy from the U.S. Army and his wife. They currently live in North Carolina. He had been stationed (having her with him) in various parts of Asia over the years, but never (not surprisingly, since he is in his mid-forties) in Vietnam, so they were seeing it for the first time. He was a fun and interesting guy.

At around 8 p.m. Linda and I took off in search of a place to eat. In doing so, we strolled past a place with young, sexy, barely dressed Vietnamese girls; a strip club?! I was showing more interest than Linda wanted me to, but it was purely academic, really! I mean, strip clubs in a Communist country? Today, I asked Hieu if strip clubs are allowed in Vietnam. Oh no, they aren't he says. Those aren't strip clubs, the girls, he says, "don't get totally undressed!" Oh, well thank goodness for that! At least I didn't miss anything when Linda drug me away by the ear.

We had a few glasses of wine at a pretty classy wine bar and then went walking in search of an Italian restaurant. We found it, we ate it and then we went to bed. We had a 6 a.m. wake-up call for our trek to Chau Doc to be ready for!

HCMC is much more westernized than anything else we have seen thus far in Vietnam. I wasn't really surprised at that since I understood that the Communist government has allowed some of the capitalistic roots of HCMC established during the American War to remain, but I was surprised that HCMC has as much interest and character as it has. It's true I had only a limited view since I was there only on for twelve waking hours. HCMC is Hanoi with a capitalistic twist, and I enjoyed it more than I thought I would.

Well, if I ever am going to get malaria, it will be from tonight. I am sitting on a deck just a few meters above the Mekong River in Chau Doc on an otherwise gorgeous evening. I was being swarmed by mosquitos. The waiter saw me (I am the only person dumb enough to be outdoors) and scooted a bowl over to me; like a stand-up ashtray with liquid in the bowl. I thought he was going to light it, but he showed me a swab and indicated I was supposed to spread the liquid over my exposed skin. Well, I doused myself with this lemongrass oil, and those little buzzing bastards don't like me anymore. The bad news is that after swabbing my leg I saw that the swab was covered in blood. It was mosquito blood, that is, my blood, from inside the mosquitos I inadvertently squished against my skin applying the oil. Great!

I love rivers. And the Mekong is one of the world's great ones. And like all of the great ones, a working facility. I was mesmerized driving along it today on our way here. Watching the old clunker boats plying the waters navigating the narrow, jungled parts of the river. If anyone ever reads any of my journals, they will roll their eyes as I go on and on with how enthralling I think river activity is. The Mekong competes with the Danube and Bangkok's Chao Praya as one of the best. As I sit here now in the calm of the evening I can hear long-tail boats churn up or down the river; I can't tell which because it is too dark to see and the boats don't have running lights!

This morning when we left the Grand Hotel in HCMC, Hieu and our driver drove us first to My Tho about two hours away. At My Tho, we took a little river cruise on the Mekong River. We stopped at a place to sample some of the tropical fruits from the area, most of which we had tried before, but not all. We then left that boat and hopped into a sampan paddled by two women. They rowed us to a house up a tight little waterway where a

farmer had bee hives for making honey. It was pretty cool to push my finger into the hive covered---and I mean covered---with bees. I sampled the honey straight from my honey-covered finger. I thought that was really cool. We sat down and had tea with honey and ginger and some nut candy they also made at this little farm (or maybe, swamp) house in the middle of nowhere next to a canal in the marshlands of the Mekong Delta. It was fun.

From there, we boarded another boat to another island, Ben Tre, which was more commercial, not tour bus commercial, nor tour boat commercial, but you could see it was all set up to receive tourists like us. At Ben Tre they make candy, taffy actually. None of it really interested us, so we moved on to the horse-carriage ride. It was more like a horse-drawn wagon and when I saw it I thought to myself, okay, now we are talking tourist tacky. But not so much. We only traveled maybe one kilometer before U-turning. Because we traveled along this narrow, wagon-wide lane, it ended up being an up close and personal kind of experience with local, countryside life. I wish it would have lasted longer! Knowing I had scoffed at this ride when I read about it on our itinerary, I chastised myself after thinking I need to learn that any travel experience can be a good one if you keep your mind open to it.

From there we boated back to our car and started the 4½ hour drive to Chau Doc, where I am now. We crossed a dozen or more bridges and took two ferries to navigate across the delta and to the Cambodian border. There were some great things to see and it was a great drive, but long. I was ready to get out of the car when we arrived at this beautiful Victoria Hotel here in Chau Doc. And I did, but not for long.

I soon got back into the car for the last part of the day's organized activities. We were off to Nui Sam, or Sam Mountain. A ½-hour drive to the top of the only hill within about a billion miles. Nui Sam is right on the border with Cambodia and it is as flat as you can imagine all around it. From the top of the mountain (hill, really), it was a beautiful view of thousands of acres of rice fields, and not far away was the village of Chau Doc. It was about 4:30 p.m. when we were driving up the narrow two kilometer road from the bottom to the top. Along the way, we encountered a whole bunch of locals walking along the road to the top of the hill for exercise; and it would be exercise. It is not an easy trek. I thought it was nice to see old and young alike exercising like that.

No exercise for me, though. When I got back to the hotel in Chau Doc I changed into my swimsuit and jumped into the hotel's pool---and then I jumped out, went to the lounge chair next to the river and ordered a beer. Except for taking a break for a shower, I have been sitting here since, watching the river action, drinking my beer(s), catching up in my journal and relaxing. And since I mosquito-proofed myself, it has been wonderfully relaxing and pleasant here by the pool, which literally juts out over the river. Gorgeous.

Linda just came out and shattered my poolside reverie by telling me she had checked emails and had heard from Britt. Someone broke into their house and robbed them last night. I feel bad for them; what a horrible feeling that is.

FRIDAY, DECEMBER 15

A woman on the Mekong River near Chau Doc

Yesterday, when we were at the farmer's house on the island sampling honey, we also sampled the rice wine he made. Much like a shot of whiskey. Hieu says it won't give you a hang-over like whiskey will because it is made from rice. I didn't intend to find out.

I am at the Victoria Chau Doc getting ready to leave on a boating excursion. We have several more of these over the next two days.

——— ——— ———

Wow, another great day! And we aren't done. I am sitting at the Victoria Hotel in Can Tho. We arrived here around 2 p.m. and we leave again at 4 p.m., about fifteen minutes from now. After we arrived we checked in to the hotel, freshened up, and wrote emails home. Then, I took time for a massage. When we leave here in a few minutes, we will tour downtown Can Tho and then go on a river cruise on the Mekong.

This is the email I wrote home:

CAN THO, VIETNAM
Subject: Reporting from the Mekong Delta

Hi everyone! All is well with us; we are back on the track of actually doing something after 5 days of beach time and 2 days of ducking the bad-weather remnants of Typhoon Durian. We missed Durian to the north and Typhoon Utor to the south...good ole Mother Nature is having trouble tracking us this trip. If you heard of Utor, she/he/it took a turn north at the last minute so our weather in the Mekong Delta is ..... sweltering. No, that is NOT me complaining.

We only had a day in Ho Chi Minh City, but saw a lot. We drove through the same gate the tank did on April 30, 1975 (we at least opened it first, he drove over it)....the world renowned photo of the North's take over. And we saw the room where the captain of that tank "captured" the South Vietnamese government, who were sitting in the cabinet room, probably a little nervously, waiting to hand over the keys to their country. We also saw the US Embassy, the building that is generally thought to be the one from "Miss Saigon"; that image of panicked people climbing stairs on top of the building to try to get into the last US helicopter to leave Vietnam. All history, but recent enough to have its impact....at least on me.

We left Ho Chi Minh City yesterday morning and have been seeing some very cool things here in the Delta. We have somehow done a good job of getting away from touristy areas and have been having some very rewarding up-close-and-personal contact with local Vietnamese to see how they live. They seem to enjoy sharing and are very welcoming of us. And although I see to it that some Vietnamese dong finds its way into their hands, they rarely have their hands out.

We over-nighted last night on a branch of the Mekong River very near the Cambodian border in a town called Chau Doc, and have been touring the Delta today. We have more yet to do today, we just had a brief respite here in Can Tho between excursions so I thought I would let you know we are ok. Tomorrow we end up the day in Ho Chi Minh City once again, to catch a flight the following day to Laos. I will write again.

Tam Biet

Gary

This morning we caught a small long-tail boat from the dock of the Victoria Chau Doc Hotel and spent two hours touring a floating village and a Cham Village.

Our boat pulled up alongside a house in the fishing---or floating, I should say---village, got out of the long-tail and walked onto the floating fish farm. It had a living area and pens of live fish. There were seven or more submerged pens in which they raised fish from the egg. Each pen had fish of the same maturity within it but the multiple pens spanned the maturity scale, so the first one had newly born fish and the last one had fish ready for sale, generally about two pounds in size. The family was a young couple, recently married with no kids; they spoke no English. While we were there, they were both busy; the man was knelt down readying the fire in the house to cook the two fish he had cleaned and the woman had gone to the edge of the floating house dock to greet a merchant in a canoe who was selling Jack Fruit and watermelons.

She bought a melon, and then casually negotiated the narrow, irregularly placed slats that cross the pens back to the living area. She put the melon in a small refrigerator which was sitting below---get this---a flat screen TV! I noticed many of the floating houses had TV antennas, but I didn't notice the source of power. It could have been wires strung underwater to the mainland, or a generator, although I don't recall the noise of one.

For the benefit of any future-year readers of this, in the year 2006, flat screen TV's are still a wee bit of a novelty and are expensive (even by American standards) and we still know what TV antennas are (you might have to ask your ancestors); they are still seen in rural America. Technology moves pretty fast in this world, I thought I should put that in perspective.

While at the floating house, they let Linda feed the fish. She loved that, so did the fish.

We hopped back into the long-tail and puttered through the rest of the floating village seeing an amazing way of life. Impoverished, dirty (again, by our standards), but the villagers seemingly getting along well; well fed and happy.

We docked and walked ashore to a Cham village. Cham are an ancient culture in S.E. Asia and common in the Mekong Delta where they are Muslim. The Cham we saw in Central Vietnam are Buddhist. Because of river flooding, the Cham live in stilted houses, pretty ramshackle stilted houses.

At one of our stops in the village, we watched a girl working a silk loom. It was amazing how rickety the loom was and how beautiful the woven result was. Who the hell crafted the loom in the first place? Complicated contraption, even this archaic one.

We got back to the Victoria Hotel in Chau Doc, checked out and took off down river in the car around 10 a.m. toward Can Tho.

I have been on a serious mission to get a photograph of two or three school girls riding their bicycles. Now, before you start thinking I am some sort of a pervert, the school girls wear all white (generally) garments called the ao dai, usually with a hat, which preferably for the sake of my photograph will be the traditional conical hat.

The ao dai (pronounced ow-yai in the South and ow-zai in the North) is the national dress of Vietnam and was designed surprisingly (to me) recently in the 1930's. The ao dai is very practical for the Vietnamese, as intended by the designer. It maintains modesty but allows ventilation and freedom of movement; it doesn't wrinkle and dries quickly. That said, it covers everything, but its gossamer-thin fabric hides almost nothing---it is very demure and provocative.

I had seen the image over and over of girls on bicycles with the long white ao dai and their dark ponytails emerging from under their conical hats---to me, the quintessential Vietnamese image. I wanted to capture it with my camera, badly. Another image is of the elderly woman (see, I am an equal-opportunity pervert) carrying fruit in the baskets hanging from both ends of the bar sitting atop their shoulders.

Anyway, I made the driver stop twice during our drive today trying to get the school-girl photo, and I am still not satisfied.

We made two other stops during our drive. One to see an incense-making operation and the other to see an alligator farm. You would think the incense sticks you buy for a penny would be mass produced in factories; maybe elsewhere, but not in Vietnam. It is mind-boggling to walk into a house and see three women making incense sticks at an incredible rate, and with only the most primitive tools in dirt-poor surroundings.

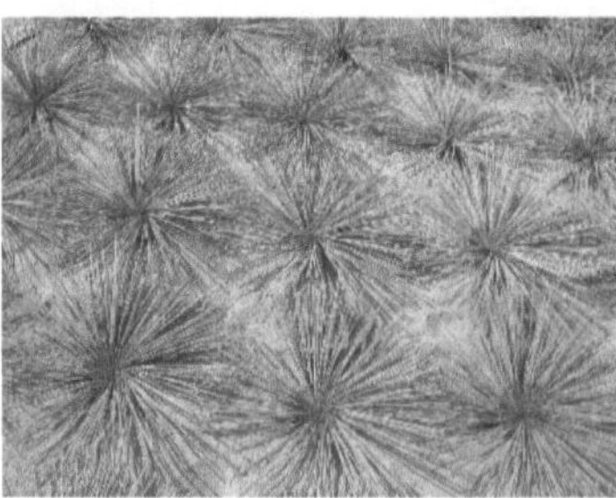

At the house at which we stopped, there was a three-year-old girl, or so, just as cute as could be. I made sure to ask the adults if I could include her in the pictures I took; the women kindly agreed. When we were about to leave, I asked Hieu if it was appropriate to leave them some money. He hesitated clearly thinking it wasn't. So, I suggested maybe I just give something to the little girl. He agreed, so I pulled 10,000 dong ($.60) from my pocket, handed Hieu my camera and motioned permission for me to have my photo taken with her. The three women and two men in the place by now had stopped working and were watching what I was doing. I kneel and ask, again using motions, the little girl to stand next to me. Shyly, she nods, moves in next to me and Hieu takes the photo. I showed the little girl the picture on the digital read-out on the back of the camera and then showed it to the adults. Everyone is smiling, thinking (I hope) that I am the great American---and then I blow it.

I patted the little girl on the head. A Buddhist, which they all are, would have taken more kindly to me patting her on the butt. The head to them is strictly off limits. I knew that, but my action was instinctual. I jerked my hand back when I belatedly realized my faux paus. My quick action startled the girl, who was too young to have learned the customs of her religion or to have thought my gesture a gaff. I moved away making all the apologetic motions I could muster to the adults, who, frankly, despite my horror seemed to understand that I meant no disrespect.

Hieu, seeing my self-disgust as we walked toward the car assured me it was okay, that my action wasn't that much of a taboo with children. But sensing that his assurances didn't really mollify me, Hieu walked back into the house and said all the right things (I presume) on my behalf. When I was having a beer with him later he told me how much he and the adults in the house appreciated my concern and respected me for caring. But, I cast a shadow on a perfectly grand moment and it aggravates me. From great American to great American idiot!

As we drove southeasterly toward Can Tho, we stopped in Long Xuyen at an alligator farm. In large pens labelled from A to E are hundreds, if not thousands, of alligators ranging from small (A) to very large (E). These alligators are harvested for their hides to make belts and purses. Standing next to the chicken wire fence separating the C's from us, an alligator suddenly lurched at Linda hitting the fence. I

don't know what prevented Linda from wetting her pants, because I damned near did! In the pens labelled 1 – 5 there were alligators that were being raised to be sold as meat. There was no apparent difference in size in the five pens, but I gather they were given different diets. What flavor of gator would you like today?

As we were getting ready to leave the alligator farm, we were taking turns using the restroom. There were four teenage girls (with a similar aged boy) filling a doorway watching us. The girls said something to Hieu; they told him they thought I was "very handsome" and that I looked like Bill Clinton. They love Bill Clinton in Vietnam so their association of me with him is always positive. It dawns on me that it is a good thing I don't look like Richard Nixon! The girls were "university" students (meaning age 16-17) from HCMC. They were visiting their friend whose family owns the alligator farm. They spoke English very well. We talked for a while and I took a picture of them before leaving.

SATURDAY, DECEMBER 16

Floating market at Cai Rang in the Mekong Delta

We had an early morning this morning, leaving the Victoria Can Tho Hotel at 6:30 this morning to catch a boat to observe the floating market at Cai Rang. It was a great experience, weaving through closely packed boats, some moving, some not. It caused to me to turn to Linda and say that it reminded me of my buddy Chuck weaving through boats at Seafair on Lake Washington. The market is quite an affair; families (including the family rooster on many of the boats) hawking their wares and goods from the very boat on which they live, moving among each other to buy, sell or trade goods, mostly fruit and vegetables at this market. I hope the pictures I took give some idea of how crazy and interesting this market was.

After the floating market, we boated to a dock, hopped off and saw a rice mill (unscheduled) and a family farm where rice paper and vermicelli (a thin form of rice noodle) is made. At the rice mill a line of men were packing rice bags out to a truck. When they saw me, they all started saying "Bill Clinton"; two even came up and shook my hand! As I walked on, down the lane from the mill to the farm, I started feeling less like a "monkey at the zoo" and more like how a large-breasted woman must feel. People were stopping in their tracks and gawking. This Bill Clinton thing is getting out of control!

The rice paper making process was interesting and, again, amazing in how primitive the surroundings are. It is hard to believe the rice paper we eat most every meal here in Vietnam comes from places like the one we saw; but it does.

Linda selects the damnedest places to announce she needs a bathroom...."Now!" I look at her like she is nuts.

Can't she see that any bathroom experience at this moment will not be a pleasant one? Apparently not. Hieu asks the lady of the farm who then leads Linda and Hieu out into the bush, quickly getting out of sight. I fully expected this not to turn out well. I was right. "Gary!" I rush out through the bush to the river's edge where she and Hieu are standing looking at two small tree trunks jutting out horizontally over the water from the river bank. There is a little tarped-off area at the end of the poles: the bathroom. The idea is that you walk, balancing on the parallel tree trunks, to get behind the tarp and with one foot on each pole, squat, do your business between the poles into the water (bottled water, anyone?). "Very clean", Hieu kept repeating, "very clean", as if he expected this American lady with "special finger nails" to actually attempt using this device! She didn't.

On our walk back to the village from the farm, Hieu asked a woman in a house we happened to pass by if she had a "toilet" that Linda could use. She did and was kind enough to allow this complete stranger into her humble little hut to use it. She would not accept any money, either. As Hieu and I waited outside the hut for Linda, we talked to the grandpa of the house who was proudly putting the finishing touches on a rolling high chair that he had made for his grandson. I took a picture.

SUNDAY, DECEMBER 17

Saigon River from the rooftop bar of the Majestic Hotel in HCMC

Linda and I are having coffee and breakfast sitting in the Majestic Hotel in HCMC at the hotel's fifth floor rooftop outdoor café that overlooks the Saigon River---did I ever mention how much I like rivers? I could watch this river activity for hours. Right now, there are three ferries constantly shuttling back and forth across the river, so far successfully avoiding each other and the very heavy up and down river barge, tug and hydrofoil traffic. Very fun to watch. And the weather today in HCMC is gorgeous!

We leave HCMC at noon today for the airport to catch a 2 p.m. flight to Vientiane, Laos---the next chapter of this excursion. Linda and I noted a little discrepancy in our schedule---I missed a day! Our flight out of Hanoi to go home next week leaves around midnight the 23rd and I failed to make a hotel reservation for the night of the 22nd. It isn't a big deal, we will add a night in Hanoi.

I sent the following group email home today:

HO CHI MINH CITY, VIETNAM
Subject: On our way to Laos

Hello again. We are well and all is going great!

We are currently in Ho Chi Minh City and leave in a couple of hours for Laos, the next chapter of this excursion.

We really enjoyed the Mekong Delta portion of our trip. We spent a lot of time on the river, seeing villages, floating markets and other things. We stopped by an alligator farm yesterday. Thousands of alligators in pens labeled A to E, according to size...the E's are huge. Standing next to the chicken wire fence of the C's, a 4-foot alligator lunged at Linda striking the fence a foot from her foot with a loud clang. From the tree 10 yards away where she landed, Linda glared at the gator and made some comment about needing a new purse. The gator quickly slithered back into the water.

I get a lot of attention in this country. My size and gray hair are part of it, but the fact I look like Bill Clinton to them, they really take notice. Daily I hear comments about Mr. Clinton. The good news is, they love Bill in this country (maybe cause he ducked the war), so therefore they like me! Thank God I don't look like Richard Nixon!

Unlike from what I am hearing of Seattle weather, the weather here has been incredibly good. Hope all of you have survived the weather there without damage.

I will try to write from Laos.

Gary

Yesterday, after Linda's potty break, we boated back to Can Tho, checked out of the Victoria Hotel and drove the five hours back to HCMC. During this time, I started sneezing and getting a runny nose. Once we got to HCMC and checked into the Majestic Hotel, Linda and I went for a walk and I started getting worse. In fact, the sneezing and dripping nose was really irritating me. I went back to the Majestic Hotel, worked out in their gym and got a massage after taking some drugs. I felt better for a while, but then miserable again later while Linda and I were having wine and dinner. I went back to the hotel early, crashed and let myself sleep in this morning. So far today, I feel good.

My dripping nose may have been caused by an allergic reaction due to an impromptu stop I insisted we make yesterday. On our drive from Can Tho, I had the driver stop at a factory we passed. It was an impulse thing, I didn't even know what the factory was. We did a U-turn and I hopped out of the car to check it out. It turned out to be a rice processing factory. I strolled in looking around the factory, trying to understand the process, asking questions, inhaling the dusty air, and apparently, once again, looking like Bill Clinton.

The whole place shut down as the workers moved away from their work stations to greet me. I am reasonably convinced they thought I actually was Bill Clinton; there was no one there to tell them otherwise. They insisted a photo be taken---assuming I suspect their faces might end up in the Oval Office.

When Linda and I went out last night, we first went to the same wine bar we liked when we were in HCMC a few nights ago and were greeted by the familiar faces of the bartenders and waitresses, as well as the owner, Stella, who insisted we sit down and enjoy a free drink. She was having a private party that night for her regular customers. A very, energetic, tiny Vietnamese woman, she owns five bar/restaurants, two in HCMC, one in Hong Kong and two in Bangkok. Amazingly, we have been to one of her Bangkok restaurants, Monsoon! She was having "traffic night", her staff was dressed as traffic cops and she was handing out colored tags to everyone. Green if you are available and red if you aren't. She would also write little quips on the cards, "Take me home", "I'm easy, but not cheap", "Don't call me, I'll call you". She and Linda were having fun coming up with others. I had my own, "I miss Monica." Stella and her friend, an Englishman (Linda and I weren't sure if they were married), understood my little Bill Clinton quip and suggested I add something about wanting a cigar!

Linda and I left the party and went next door for a Thai dinner intending to come back to resume the party when we had finished eating. But, I was not feeling that well, in fact, I was miserable. I told Linda to go party without me, I needed a bed. She did, but didn't stay long (I forgot to give her money!). I was dead asleep when she got back to the hotel room not much later.

—— —— ——

I am now sitting in the Pochentong Airport at Phnom Penh, Cambodia. Man, it is beautiful, maybe the nicest airport I have ever been in! I didn't even know we were stopping in Phnom Penh, let alone deplaning. Oops, re-boarding now, gotta go!

MONDAY, DECEMBER 18

The Lao Plaza Hotel in Vientiane decorated for Christmas

I am having breakfast at the Lao Plaza Hotel in Vientiane, Laos. It is clear weather and comfortably cool at around 75 degrees.

We will see some sights in Vientiane this morning then catch a 12:30 p.m. flight to Luang Prabang, probably about on hour-long flight.

We landed in Vientiane at 5 p.m. yesterday, and took a short drive with our guide and driver around town seeing the Mekong River waterfront. We got dropped off at the Lao Plaza Hotel, got checked in and Linda and I were back out walking around town by 6 p.m.

Vientiane is the laid-capital of Laos. It has a population of 150,000 and sits on the Mekong River which forms the border with Thailand. After the busy-ness of Vietnam, it is quite a change to walk through Laos' biggest city and see so few people and cars and motorcycles. It is like a different world here, quiet and peaceful.

We walked down to the waterfront and came across an outdoor women's aerobics class, music blaring and women in exercise clothes following the rather hot, female instructor. There were probably thirty women, some with kids, dancing along with the tunes.

We found a pleasantly busy bar and sat and practiced Laotian with the bartender. Soon, we left the bar and walked about six blocks to That Dam, a large black stupa, not to see the stupa, but rather to go to the wine café located there. It was a great little café with good wine and awesome outdoor seating, and it served hamburgers! We had gone there because the Lonely Planet guidebook said it had great Lao food---wrong. We had a nice glass of wine and practiced more Lao with the very helpful waiter and then walked off to find Laotian food in the general direction he pointed us.

We ended up at Sua Lao, which our guide had recommended earlier. It was very good food, but spicier than I could tolerate. I was a little fooled, not expecting Lao food to be that spicy, so I gobbled several bites down before I realized it was over the top for me. I ended up not eating much.

But my bigger problem at the moment had less to do with burning lips and more to do with currency. I failed to remember from the guide books that even though there are fewer kip (10,000) to the U.S. dollar than Vietnamese dong (16,000), to which I had become accustomed, the Laotians don't print bills bigger than 20,000 kip, and those large bills aren't common. So, when I went earlier to exchange $100 US, I got a full inch and a half of 10,000 kip bills, obviously, 100 of them! When I was handed the wad of money, I realized too late my mistake; I forgot my plan to get very little kip since U.S. currency is commonly accepted in Laos. Linda, noting the look of dismay on my face when I saw what the cashier was handing me, howled. Sitting in the restaurant, it took me a while to sort through the pile of kip.

We strolled back to our hotel in the pleasant evening and went to bed around 11 p.m.

There are some newly constructed things in Vientiane but mostly things are just under construction; everything is an incomplete project it seems, streets, curbs, underground utilities, buildings, everything. I am not sure if it is a sign that good things are happening here or that nothing ever gets completed.

We have seen more Americans in the fifteen hours in Vientiane than the entire prior three weeks in Vietnam. Not sure why that would be. It is possible I guess that we are just seeing the same Americans over and over again; maybe I should pay more attention. It is, for sure, though, that we are seeing plenty of Christmas decorations and getting earfuls of cheesy Christmas music---like right now, Frosty the Snowman. Goes well with my breakfast.

The Lao language is similar to Thai, which both helps us and confuses us. And I am happy to say that Laotians wai (a greeting consisting of a slight bow, with the palms pressed together in a prayer-like fashion). It is not as consistently seen here as in Thailand, but it is a gracious greeting; one we have learned to appreciate and we are happy to see it here.

——— ——— ———

Now we are sitting at Wattay Airport in Vientiane awaiting our delayed flight to Luang Prabang. It is now noon.

After breakfast this morning, we left Lao Plaza Hotel with Slard (pronounced "Salat"), our guide. We first went to see the Wat Si Saket. Built in 1818 it is Vientiane's oldest surviving temple. We then walked across the street to the Haw Pha Kaew, a temple built to hold the Emerald Buddha in 1565. The Emerald Buddha was stolen by the Siamese in 1779 and placed in Bangkok's Wat Phra Kaew where we saw it two years ago. From there, we drove to Phat That Luang, the national symbol of Laos, which is a huge gold stupa. It was originally built in 300 B.C. to purportedly hold Buddha's breastbone. The structure has been destroyed several times in history so what we see today is a 1935 re-construction. After that, we were off to Pratuxai ("Victory Gate"). Reminiscent off the Arc de Triomphe in Paris, Pratuxai was built in 1958-60 with American money in honor of wars past. It is interesting to hear Laotians talk about the years they were controlled by the U.S.

While true, I am sure little of our literature describes it that way. With time still before getting to the airport (it is nice to be somewhere you can cover a five kilometer distance in minutes rather than an hour!), we went to the "morning market", which is open all day but is different than the "evening market", which is open---you guessed it---all day! It was a fun and active morning; we saw more of Vientiane than we expected to.

Slard is 21 years old. He comes from a tiny village along the Mekong River northwest of Vientiane. He was a novice monk for five years and has been a guide for four. Pretty impressive young man. We asked if he had a girlfriend; he laughed bashfully and said, "No, I am trying, but she is too pretty!" Funny. He lives in a dormitory since he is a student. He loved Linda's eyes and thought she was very smart. He was impressed with how "big, strong and athletic" I am. Oddly, smart was not one of the adjectives he attached to me. We spent too little time with him and he clearly felt the same way, hugging Linda at the airport like he didn't want to let her go. He did say he sees very few American tourists in Laos, which is odd because I thought I had seen so many!

Walking around today I found myself missing Hieu constantly telling me to "watch your head"; to the point I started saying it to Linda. She immediately caught the humor. It is true, I am constantly ducking in Asia, but I didn't realize how often Hieu must have said it to me. He was about Linda's height, so it is surprising he was even aware of my "head issues". "Watch your head" may become the trademark slogan of this trip.

——— ——— ———

This afternoon after getting to our Luang Prabang hotel, I took the time to shoot off an email home:

LUANG PRABANG, LAOS
Subject: Laos

Sabaai dii --

New country ... new language. Another tonal language....Vietnamese was impossible with 5 tones...we have moved up to six in Laos...BUT, the language is similar to Thai, so that helps.....not.

Ah...and then there is ordering food. Always a huge question when the menu has pictures....not a good sign. But when you are looking at the pictures and thinking what the.....???? Oh, fried grasshoppers, boiled larvae and stuffed frog....alrighty then, "Hey honey, does the broiled calf's tongue look good to you?"

We spent a quiet and wonderful night in Vientiane, Laos last night and got to Luang Prabang, Laos today where we spend the next four nights. Boating up the Mekong tomorrow for a day trip...should be fun.

Just had a few minutes and wanted to let you all know things are good here. Off to ... ah, dinner, unfortunately.....trying pig's tail tonight. Just kidding about the food thing.... although all of those goodies I mention are, indeed, available....and pictured...but the other menu options are similar to Thai...and very good. So, Gary is still eating well.

Phop kan mai!

Gary

TUESDAY, DECEMBER 19

Luang Prabang with the Mekong River from the top of Phu Si Hill

I am having morning coffee at our Luang Prabang hotel. There is some fog and cool air about this morning. The fog is burning off, but I suspect the first portion of our scheduled boat ride this morning will be a bit chilly.

Our thirty-five minute flight and transfer through the Luang Prabang airport yesterday was a breeze. We met our young female Laotian guide, Wattanay, and driver as we exited the airport. We drove straight to the Grand Luang Prabang Hotel, which is, unfortunately, four kilometers south of the town. We checked in and headed out again with Wattanay and our driver to see the sights. There is no traffic to speak of in this small town of 40,000, but the first one-half of the road into town from the hotel is very rough, so it is slow going.

Wattanay took us to two Wats: Wisunarat and Aham; they are right next to each other. The first one has Luang Prabang's oldest Buddha, he is over 500 years old. And biggest; his head touches the top of the sim (temple). The sim of the second wat was reconstructed more recently

and has drawings on its wall telling Buddha's story. Wattanay described this all to us in general and then pointed to a series of drawings that she said depicted the five sins of Buddhism: killing, robbing, drinking alcohol, adultery and a fifth one I don't recall (I have never been good with remembering no-no's). She must have seen something in my face because she smiled and said, "It's okay to drink a little alcohol." Never missing an opportunity, I said "Then a little adultery must be alright, too?" She laughed and nodded, "It is hard to live without sin." Boy, she got that right!

After some discussion, it was decided that I would walk to the top of a 500-foot hill in the middle of Luang Prabang called Phu Si (pronounced "pussy") and Linda and Wattanay would go shopping; we would meet at a bar on the other side of Phu Si in a little over an hour, or 5:45 p.m.

Phu Si has 350 stairs that gets you to its top; it is where people gather to watch and photograph the sunset; about 150 of them, in fact. The small area on top was crowded with sunset gazers; the small area not being big enough to whisk away the body odors resulting from the strenuous hike up the hill. I decided to stay for the sunset; I would be a half-hour late meeting the girls, but I figured that would be okay. The sunset was just another beautiful sunset and the French woman with whom I offered to share my bench for photo taking was just another beautiful woman! Not really beautiful, but cute, and most importantly, she didn't stink! She and I talked as we waited for the sun to set. After it had, I stepped off the bench to start the downhill trek and told her I was off to a bar (for a sinful drink). I think she wanted me to ask her along, I think I forgot to mention I have a wife---but I do, and I met her at the bar as planned.

Linda didn't have an issue with me being late, but I found out that poor Wattanay had been worried sick about me. We made plans to meet her the following morning (this morning) for our boat excursion and then she took off to go home. Left to our own, Linda and I walked the night market. They close down the main street in Luang Prabang and line it with tribal merchants selling their village's goods: silks, leathers and many other things. Really nice stuff, in general. Linda bought a long-sleeved shirt for today (which she will need) and she led me to a wine bar she had seen while I was talking to my, by now, long-lost French girlfriend from atop Phu Si.

Once we got seated, Linda immediately started chatting with a couple near our street side table. They were a thirty-ish French couple from Marseille travelling for five months through Southeast Asia. He looked like a roguish Moroccan pirate and she was just stunning. I know, I know, I am on a French woman roll. She was tall, slender, elegant and pretty---with a back pack. Pretty hot, huh? We had a great conversation with them, about travel mostly. When they got up to leave she kissed me on both cheeks. I told her that is how the French say goodbye, here is how Americans do it---and kissed her on the lips. It must have been the sinful alcohol! Fortunately, she loved it and he didn't seem to mind. Linda just shook her head.

Linda and I had a chilly tuk-tuk ride back to our hotel a couple miles out of town where we were scheduled to have dinner; a dinner paid for by BA Tours. Our hotel is one of the nicest ones around, I understand, but it is isolated and not that nice. Except for the business group that is here, we seem to be the only guests. They had a premier table set up for us at 8:30 p.m., outside overloo

king the Mekong River. It was their best table because there was no one else in the restaurant!

The problem was that it was cold. The restaurant had no indoor seating, which is odd, because we are not in the tropics here. We apologized and said there is no way we can sit outside, it was too cold. So, they moved us to what they call a bar but was more like a sitting room. Still, we were the only people. It felt like we had the entire resort to ourselves with the whole staff attending to us. This is just not our deal; we want people around! But the staff was fun and we made the best of it.

WEDNESDAY, DECEMBER 20

Linda walks down steep steps to board our boat for a trip up the Mekong River from Luang Prabang

The boat ride yesterday was awesome. We donned sweatshirts early on, but soon removed them as the day progressively got warmer. It took two hours to get upriver to our destination and less than one hour to get back. The boat was 50 feet long and 5 feet wide; Linda, Wattanay and I were the only people aboard along with the driver. It was smooth and comfortable; we moved along at 15 knots or so and enjoyed the sights.

The Mekong River is 2,700 miles long and has no dams for the last 2,000 miles, so the water level varies dramatically, by at least 30 feet from dry to wet season! It is dry season now so the water is low and all along the banks, Laotians have created temporary farms, in some cases, with huts, all of which will get washed away next May-June when the rainy season comes. Since claim to this "free" land is first-come-first-served, fences and huts are erected temporarily to perfect the farmer's claim for that plot of land for that dry season. I wonder what the protocol is for claiming land when the river first starts to recede. Interesting stuff.

We saw no wildlife or birdlife, none. Wattanay claims this is because the Laotians eat anything and everything that moves. That claim is actually backed up by the guidebooks. The mountains and jungles still have wildlife, but apparently none along the river. I find it hard to believe only because there are so few people in Lao, particularly outside of the towns. We would go for ten to fifteen minute stretches on the boat and see no living thing, no farmer, no fisherman, nothing.

We stopped at the Pak Ou Caves, 25 kilometers upriver from Luang Prabang. Except for the exercise of climbing from the shoreline to the caves (which Linda did!), there was nothing notable about them.

Linda had walked ahead of Wattanay and me in the lower cave when a cute, meek, non-Asian lady of 30 or so asked me if she could ask Wattanay a question. A tourist herself, she recognized Wattanay was likely my guide. The three of us stood around this altar in the cave where you shake a stick from a can, read the number on the stick that you have "randomly" selected and read the corresponding horoscope, written in Laotian. The girl had done all of this and wanted Wattanay to read her horoscope. The girl's eyes widened when Wattanay read horoscope. It said "you have recently lost your lover". Because of her reaction, Wattanay and I questioned her; yes, she shyly admitted that she had, in fact, dumped her boyfriend. To Wattanay's huge delight, the girl's horror and my amusement, the horoscope went on to say that she would not be able to resist the temptation of a temporary illicit relationship---very soon! She thanked us, and as Wattanay and I walked away, we both noted she was nervously looking around, checking out all the men in the cave.

From the caves we went further upriver to Ban Muang Keo, a village selected by Wattanay for us and other of her clients because it maintains its traditional way and is not accustomed to tourists. It was a phenomenal stop. It was comparable to being invited into a Lao home.

At the village we saw the equipment and process of making rice whiskey, the jars and fermentation containers were sitting under a house (the houses are stilted to protect against river flooding). The owner was not around, so Wattanay showed us the process and then we tasted the product.

Surprisingly, it actually tasted good. It has a 45% alcohol content so it was, indeed, a whiskey.

Linda bought some silk thing for gifts and we just simply walked around the village. Wattanay said 200 people lived in the village, which is probably about ten people per hut.

Getting back into the boat, we left the village and motored along the foot of a sheer limestone cliff that must have jutted 1,000 feet straight up from the water's edge. It was impressive.

We rode the current back down the river to a village just outside Luang Prabang on the north side of the Khan River. They make paper at this village out of mulberry as well as weave silk. We bought some paper art of three monks with umbrellas ($2 US) and some paper sacks to use for giving wine bottles as gifts. Then, we wandered into a place where they actually make silk, starting with the butterflies, then the larvae, then the silk-enshrouded cocoon. One cocoon makes 45 feet of silk strand. All the dyes used are natural, made from lemongrass (yellow) and tamarind (red), as two examples. And as always seems to be the case, all of this was being done in a 15 foot by 20 foot dirt-floor area---essentially someone's back yard. Very, very cool.

When we got done, our car driver was at the village to meet us and take us back to our hotel. We got there just before 4 p.m. We said goodbye to Wattanay for the day. We rested, I showered, Linda emailed and we left the hotel again on the hotel bus for downtown at 5 p.m.
Linda went shopping and I got a massage that cost me only $4 US! We met at a little wine bar on Luang Prabang's main street just after 6:30 p.m.

At the wine bar I started talking with David and Ann from England. We ended up spending the whole evening with them, including dinner. She is a "pensioner" (what does that mean, exactly?) and doesn't work and he sold his business and no longer actively works. They are traveling for two months on this trip. Their deal is to buy plane tickets to somewhere and then buy a guidebook at the airport and go from there. When they left England two weeks ago, they had no intention of going to Laos, they just ended up here. What an interesting way to travel; I would love to try that sometime.

I've been writing while sitting having morning coffee at our hotel in Luang Prabang. It is time now to go exploring.

——— ——— ———

It's now 5 p.m. We toured around all morning and then said goodbye to Wattanay around 1 p.m. Since then, we have been hanging out in Luang Prabang. We rented bikes and rode every street in town. That took about 90 minutes.

Luang Prabang is an enthralling, yet comfortable, town, At 2,000 feet above sea level and encircled by mountains, the climate is cool and, except for the constant smoke from debris burning, clear and fresh. The town sits beautifully on a peninsula formed by the confluence of the Khan and Mekong Rivers. Once the capital of a far-extending kingdom and the capital of Laos until the 16th century, it is a history-rich town. In 1995 it was inscribed on the UNESCO World Heritage Site list.

After our bike rides, we each went to get massages. What a great afternoon! The weather has been perfect, maybe 78 degrees or less, no wind, perfect blue skies, just beautiful. I am sitting street side at a small café having a beer. I just finished my massage, I'm now waiting for Linda to return from hers.

This morning we saw the former palace, now a museum. It was really quite impressive and made more so by having Wattanay describe all the things we were seeing. Unlike most palaces, this one was built in 1904 and updated in 1930; all pretty recent, so it shows pretty well.

Both the Vietnamese and Lao are superstitious people. The fact that their Buddhist beliefs and superstitions have been trampled on since 1975 by the Communists may make the mystery of their superstitions burn brighter. Each of our guides has described stories, beliefs and superstitions as semi-serious and believed in by others, but I think each of them really believe the myths, too.

We also saw Luang Prabang's most beautiful wat, and it was nice, but really, just another wat. Finally, we went to a silversmith shop where they forge the silver and etch intricate designs into them, bowls, chalices, cups, even chop sticks. Unfortunately, the artists were on a lunch break so we couldn't watch them in action, but we did see how they shaped the bowls and their works-in-progress.

Hmmmm. Double hmmmm. Linda is convinced that the girl who just gave me a massage, wasn't. A girl that is. Linda went to a different place for her massage, but walked in with me to the front desk of mine to confirm I could get in and the approximate timing. Linda was still standing at the check-in desk with me when I confirmed with the young man checking me in that I would have a female masseuse. Linda went off to her massage and I went upstairs to my massage room. I was surprised when I saw the front desk guy walk into the room after I was already laying on the massage table, but assumed he had walked in to make sure things were all set. I just laid my head back down and relaxed. The door re-opened and I glanced up to see the boyish-looking girl who was there to give me my massage. Wait, is she wearing the same clothes as that guy? Is it a uniform they all wear? She said something, I looked at her more closely. It's a girl, pretty face, short hair, no breasts, just like most of the Laotian girls. The massage was great. It was when I walked out to pay, and saw the same boy there to collect. Hmmm, sure looks like that girl masseuse. Same clothes, and no, they don't wear uniforms. Hmmm.

Linda got way too much of a kick out of that.

THURSDAY, DECEMBER 21

Monks stream by receiving alms from locals in Luang Prabang

It is 7 a.m. and I just finished feeding the Monks. That's right, the Monks, not the monkeys. I got up at 5:30 a.m. and took a tuk-tuk bus into Luang Prabang. It was freezing, probably not quite, maybe in the forties, but I was wearing shorts and sandals, totally inadequate. The Monks start their walk at 6:30 a.m. They walk through the village with food baskets slung around their necks; villagers put food in the baskets as the Monks walk by. It ends up looking like a very long receiving line. Much of the food given is rice, which the donor scoops up with his or her fingers and puts into the Monk's basket, so the Monk's food ends up having been touched by scores, if not hundreds, of hands! To me, this all seems pretty humiliating to the Monks, but it is the way their system is set up and they have been doing it for centuries.

Damn, my fingers are cold, I can hardly write.

When I first got downtown a group of men from Bangkok spied me, could see I was at a loss for what to do and asked if I wanted to join them giving alms to the Monks (and here I thought I was just feeding them!). The men spoke Thai and several spoke English. Laotians and Thais can more or less understand each other. So, these Thai men talked to some local women merchants and got themselves and me set up with baskets of sticky rice and some other things to hand out. It cost me $3 US. There were six Thai men all about my age. They were fun and funny and very gracious to invite me to join them....and to save me. As I was handing out food, some women (I thought they were simply helpful villagers) kept re-filling my basket as I emptied mine giving alms out to the passing Monks. When one of the Thai men noticed what was happening, he said, “Gary, do you understand you have to pay them for that?” I felt really stupid telling him that I thought they were just being nice. Naïve American tourists! He chastised the women in their language for taking advantage of me, so I got away with paying one of them $1 US and ignoring the rest who may or may not have given me stuff, I really hadn’t been paying attention. The Thai men thought that was pretty funny. We all had a good laugh.

Today is the shortest day of the year. Now we can look forward to longer and longer days for the next six months, provided we stay north of the equator.

I have now gotten back to the hotel. The return tuk-tuk

bus ride from town was no warmer than the ride an hour or two earlier into town. It was damned chilly. I have had some breakfast and some coffee and have warmed up, at least a little.

FRIDAY, DECEMBER 22

Down river from Kuang Si Falls near Luang Prabang

I am writing from the Melia Hotel in Hanoi, our last stop on this month-long adventure. We leave for home tomorrow at midnight.

Yesterday after my alms-giving to the Monks, Wattanay picked Linda and me up from the hotel and we drove off to see Kuang Si Falls. We stopped at a Hmong village along the way. We were lucky, the villagers were all dressed up for their New Year's celebration. The Hmong are

animists so it wasn't a Buddhist celebration, but whatever

their motivation, the young girls were dressed in elaborate dresses, lined up facing each other tossing tennis balls back and forth. They were practicing. When they get to the big festival in another nearby Hmong village later in the day, the ball tossing is part of a courting ritual. A boy and a girl toss a ball back and forth; if she drops it, she can't talk to him anymore. I don't know what happens if he drops it, and I am assuming there are likely times where she drops it on purpose.

We walked through the village and into two of the homes. In the first one, the man had two wives and six children, so the tiny little hut accommodated nine people. In the second hut there were ten people living there, but in that case there were three generations. The patriarch had three wives. One of his adult sons had a baby three weeks ago and when we were there, the mother was breast feeding it. Thatched roofs and dirt floors, each had one or two small fires openly burning on the floor. It is hard to imagine the mud and how they must deal with three months of almost constant hard rain during the rainy season. I hope the photos I took inside the huts turn out and give some idea of the conditions in which these villagers live.

Later we also walked through a Khamu village, but this village was close to the falls and benefitted from the tourist trade. Still simple and humble, but more wealth, even a couple of concrete houses.

The falls themselves were gorgeous. On the hike up to them, we passed a wildlife conservancy area where they had Asiatic bears and a tiger. These guys were saved as cubs due to their parents being killed. Both the bears and the tigers are endangered. The conservancy is trying to find a male mate for the now fully grown tigress. She is impressive. Only a chain link fence separated us from her and she was moving around brushing herself against the fence as we stood just feet away. Beautiful animal.

“Stop the car!” The driver and Wattanay both looked back at me in alarm. “Stop quickly!” I blurt out as I reached for the handle of the SUV’s side sliding door. The driver is frantically working the SUV over to the right shoulder, the side of the car on which I am sitting. But the constant stream of cyclists moving along in the right lane is preventing him from moving too quickly. My hand is on the door handle starting to pull back when I feel the first acrid swell start to rise from my stomach. As the driver moved to the road’s edge, my first fountain of puke just missed the door as I frantically slid it open. And even more surprising, or important, is that said fountain missed the school girls on the passing bicycles. The driver was still moving and had not even crossed over the rightmost lane yet. The second salvo came as we neared the shoulder. Despite my condition, I am very aware of the shrieking of the school kids on bicycles who are desperately---I assume---trying to avoid the gross brown spray spewing from the side of the SUV that is cutting in front of them. My foot hits the road before the SUV is stopped and I am able to get into the grass beyond the road’s shoulder to finish my business.

As I lean over hands on knees, the school-kid shrieking has morphed into the universal school-kid "ew-ing". After what was a pretty violent vomiting session, I turn back toward the SUV to ask Linda for a Kleenex and there is Wattanay standing with an opened water bottle smiling like nothing had happened. Too sick to be embarrassed, I thank her, apologize to the driver and get back into the car to finish our ride to the airport for out flight to Hanoi.

We were at the airport a couple of hours early and I tossed cookies one more time before boarding the plane. I was able to get through the flight, through immigration in Vietnam and to the Melia Hotel okay.

My stomach first started bothering me that morning on the way to see the falls and got progressively worse. When we got back to our Luang Prabang hotel about 12:30 p.m., I begged off the plan to visit the Chinatown market and went, instead, to the hotel room, took sum Tums and laid down. I didn't feel any better when I got into the SUV for the ride to the airport, but I didn't think I was anywhere close to vomiting!

When we got to the Melia Hotel from the Hanoi airport in the evening, I had to deal with the BA Tour people about paying them for the hotel upgrade and the extra night in Hanoi. Linda had refused to stay another night in the perfectly fine Hoa Binh Hotel, which had been our reliable (but, admittedly, not that great) Hanoi home off and on for the past month. I wanted to pay BA Tour by credit card to preserve my dwindling cash, but that was too confusing for them. So, I finally relented and paid in cash just to make them go away. Linda and I got checked into our swank suite at the Melia Hotel, settled in and then explored the hotel looking for something simple to eat. I looked at one menu and realized the thought of food might make me hurl again, so I left Linda on her own and went to the room and curled up in bed. It was only 8:30 p.m.

I feel good this morning, although only fruit sounded good to me, so that is all I have had.

SATURDAY, DECEMBER 23

One of those "signature" images from Vietnam

Last day!

I remember thinking when we first started this journey that this day seemed a long way away. I knew though that when I got to the point of writing "last day" I would likely have filled this leather journal up with a lot of great experiences. We surely had the experiences, I will have to read this damned thing at some point to see how I did in writing about them.

We were waken this morning at first light by the morning announcements. There is a public address system throughout Hanoi and in some (most?) other Vietnamese cities, from which announcements are made, apparently daily, but I am not sure. When I first heard an announcement, the sound reminded me of hearing a weirdo with a megaphone on a Seattle street corner. We heard these public announcements before in Vietnam's countryside, too, but in those cases the public address system was hauled around in a trailer towed by a motorcycle or in the back of a pickup truck. How any message can be received in the short amount of time it takes even a slow-moving vehicle to pass is beyond me. These are apparently public-service type of announcements, although I have to believe there is also political propaganda as well.

In one case we saw a pickup truck loaded with large speakers driving down a dirt road among the rice paddies. Our guide, Hieu, told us the announcement was advising farmers to use a new rice strain to battle a rice disease the Mekong delta has developed. I don't know what the morning announcements say in Hanoi, but this morning the announcement included music. I am going to remember to ask our driver tonight about that on the way to the airport.

Yesterday morning I spent about an hour on the computer, checking our flight tonight, doing some business and sending an email home letting everyone know we are safe and on our way home:

> ***HANOI, VIETNAM***
> *Subject: Homeward Bound*
>
> *Hello everyone....we are back in Hanoi, our last stop before boarding the plane for home tomorrow night at midnight. We will arrive Seattle at 7 am Christmas Eve day, the 24th.*
>
> *The fun and excitement has continued for us. We very much enjoyed Laos and our last stop, Luang Prabang, is the kind of place to spend a week enjoying the simple life. Very nice.*
>
> *Maybe I should have tried the fried grasshoppers. I ate something much less interesting that my tummy didn't much like and involuntarily got rid of rather quickly, throwing it all up out the side sliding door of the moving van we were in. In Southeast Asia, there is always a swarm of people moving along on foot and on bicycles in the right lane; a dangerous place to be, it turns out, if you are near a van carrying a suddenly and violently sick American. I remember the*

shrieking of school girls on bicycles swerving to (hopefully) avoid the brown liquid spewing from the side of the van which was cutting in front of them desperately trying to get to the side of the road. Anyway, more detail than you asked for....what, you didn't ask?.....but, since I am sure you are concerned, a day later I am feeling fine, thank you.

We now have two days without a lot to do in Hanoi before flying home. Gary counted the days wrong so we have two days here instead of the planned one, but that is okay, we can relax a little before getting home.

We will see you all soon.

Gary

I also took time to write Britt to thank her for all she has done. It is nuts all the little and big things she has taken care of for us while we have been gone. We will have to think of some appropriate way to show our appreciation. She is a good friend.

After my time on the computer, Linda and I took off to get some U.S. currency and hair spray (in inverse order of importance). We stopped on a busy street corner (as if there was some other kind in Hanoi) planning our next move when two vendors converged on us to sell us something. I gave them my polished Vietnamese “No, thank you’s”, but then felt one of them poking me belligerently in the back as I passed by. I wheel angrily around and see David and Anne, the English couple we had dinner with several nights ago in Luang Prabang. What a surprise! We chatted for a while then parted company.

From there I went exploring and Linda went back to our hotel. Actually, she ended up exploring some too---she got lost. My exploration lasted longer than I intended because I got lost, too. I love walking the streets, seeing the work, the play, the family life. For many of these people all this happens in the same small square of sidewalk and every step long any walk is a chance to observe them and their lives.

Linda and I had dinner last night at Emperor, a restaurant recommended by a couple from America who spotted us and talked with us in a Luang Prabang restaurant a few nights ago. The American couple was from San Francisco; they were sitting with friends of theirs from Singapore. The four of them shared with us that they had been watching Linda and me and had a bet among themselves about us. The American man had it right, we were from Seattle. The American woman had us from somewhere else in the U.S. but had me pegged as either a TV personality (I love her) or the CEO of a large company. We actually were on the same flight from Luang Prabang to Hanoi as the Singapore couple, but since I was feeling so punk, we didn't talk much.

While having dinner at Emperor, a young, well-dressed Vietnamese man came to our table and asked if we remembered him. After some explanation, it turned out he remembered Linda, not me, from waiting on us at another Hanoi restaurant where he served us when we were in Hanoi weeks ago.

After dinner, we walked into a place we had been before and four or five of the staff remembered us from a month ago. This time, three of them stood, as their work allowed, and chatted with us for quite a while, showing the typical Vietnamese curiosity and country pride.

——— ——— ———

It is now noon. Linda's stomach is bothering her so I decided to go for a walk through Hanoi's old quarter; I wanted to be sure I inhaled my fill of fumes before I get another chance to visit another Asian city. Man, it is bad. I try inhaling through my nose in hopes that my nose hairs, which badly need clipped, will filter some of the bad stuff. It is bad, but it is worth it.

The way Vietnamese work and live is foreign and incomprehensible to us, yet admirable and fascinating. As mentioned before, merchants in the old quarter of Hanoi are clustered on streets specializing in the products they

sell. It was a pleasure walking down the "stationery" street and "metal-working" street. Not surprisingly, on those streets no one is trying to stop you as you pass by to sell you something; wedding invitations and metal grills aren't exactly impulse buys. On the other hand, if you want to buy a pair of jeans, how does one decide to which one of the twenty stores on the same block you go to? Somehow it all works.

I am getting down to the last entries here. How do I wrap it all up? First, Vietnam versus Laos. The similarities are that the people of both countries seem happy and confident. Neither have anything of great material value (by our standards); both have suffered greatly from recent (twenty years) brutal pasts. People selling in both countries are constant but not aggressively persistent. A smile, a shake of the head, or a "no, thank you" gets a smile and a slight wave of acknowledgement in return. I think the Vietnamese are a more physically attractive people and have more country pride than do the Lao who are more a nation of tribes. The Lao believe in karma leading them to believe that hard work and stress will gain them nothing since they don't believe they have control over anything. Airplanes are rarely on time in Laos, little of anything occurs on schedule. The Vietnamese airlines, on the other hand, are punctual; Vietnamese live a busier, although not frenetic, lifestyle.

During our entire visit to Vietnam, we never experienced any negative reaction to our being American. In large part, that is probably because over 60% of Vietnam's population was not even alive when the American War ended in 1975. Also, in the North they seem to think in the logical terms of having won the war, so why would there be bitterness? In the South, Vietnamese are mostly thankful for all of the infrastructure built by the Americans during the fifteen years they were there. While the Vietnam War may be a recent memory for me, the American War has been mostly forgotten by the Vietnamese.

And finally, the images of this trip that will stay with me a lifetime:

> Vietnamese men squatting on their haunches, the impossible (for me) position of squatting with their butts nearly touching the ground, their feet flat to the ground and their knees to their chins.
>
> Motorcycles. No image of Vietnam is complete without a motorcycle or bicycle; or scores of them lined up side-by-side at an intersection waiting for a traffic light.
>
> A petite elderly woman with a conical hat moving in her rhythmic jaunt with two fruit-filled baskets dangling from her shoulder bar; poetry in motion, seriously.

School girls riding bicycles two and three abreast down a bustling street or road with their white ao dai uniforms flowing behind them as they talk and gesture like school girls do the world over.

A man, his plow and his water buffalo knee deep in the muddy waters of a rice field.

A man, a woman, a child and a pig in a cage---all on one motorcycle.

The provocative allure of the ao dai; that traditional dress worn by Vietnamese women

The last image is of me staring slack-jawed in awe at the wonder of each and every one of the above. What an awesome trip!

Until next time.....

Gary

www.ingramcontent.com/pod-product-compliance
Ingram Content Group UK Ltd.
Pitfield, Milton Keynes, MK11 3LW, UK
UKHW041943190726
13854UKWH00004B/1754

9 781329 193338